On Heights & Hunger

Josh MacIvor-Andersen

Outpost19 | San Francisco
outpost19.com

MacIvor-Andersen, Josh
        On Heights & Hunger/ Josh MacIvor-Andersen
        ISBN 9781944853006 (pbk)

Library of Congress Control Number: 2016910706

OUTPOST19

ORIGINAL
PROVOCATIVE
READING

On
Heights
& Hunger

For my brother, who taught me to climb.
And for Austin, who told me to write.

Table of Contents

Prologue	i
One	1
Two	5
Three	29
Four	41
Five	55
Six	59
Seven	89
Eight	113
Nine	131
Ten	148
Eleven	185
Epilogue	191

Prologue

I said the Sinner's Prayer with Mom when I was five because I loved Jesus. I think it was real love, too, because I had fed on all those New Testament healings and raisings from the dead, felt the injustice of the crucifixion, imagined the sneers of murderous hypocrites. That's what Dad always called the Pharisees: "Hypocrites."

The stories settled deep. I digested them all and they were bearing fruit, a bona fide Jesus love.

Christ's literary competitors were also a little limp. The recalcitrant bunny in *Goodnight Moon* or stubborn, uppity Max in *Where the Wild Things Are*. The Son of God was sitting on a loaded narrative throne: kindness in the midst of cruelty, a revolutionary of goodness who boldly denounced the powerful and rich and haughty. So they killed him.

And then, of course, resurrection. Dawn at the end of a dark night. I was smitten. At five-years-old I wanted Jesus in my heart, deep and settled, because it seemed like the place that was the absolute closest to me. My center. The fleshy mechanism that worked like a pump to make all my blood ebb and flow. "He could be right there," Mom said, gently touching my chest.

I took her words literally. A beautiful, intimate, interior love—forever.

But it was love shot through with fear. I was equally terrified that Mom and Dad would rocket off to heaven, having already said the Prayer, and leave me alone, perhaps sitting right there on the edge of my bunk bed (bottom mattress) where my hands were clasped tightly between Mom's. The early sermons of Christ's passion included a few caveats. I had a distinct vision of those same maternal hands—warmth, pressure, two palms pressing inward—suddenly vanished.

I'm not sure I had ever made a decision so deliberate. I loved Jesus, yes, and also felt the panicked sentiment of: *Take me with you!*

Mom was tender and serious. She knew this was a threshold, and that at five I was crossing it sincerely, little-boy eyes wide open.

So I wept and repeated after her: "I invite you, Jesus, to be my personal lord and savior, and to come into my heart and forgive my sins and fill me with your holy spirit. Amen."

I'm pretty sure that's verbatim. The most accurate dialogue I've ever written.

Then this happened: all the fear and anxiety I felt over being left alone, left with the unsaved, those who had never asked Jesus into their hearts like Dad and Mom and now me, transferred in a flash to my big brother, Aaron, who was eleven months older and kind of bad. Sometimes really bad. He had done things to me, to others, to small animals with a BB gun that were serious sins in need of forgiveness. Forgiveness I knew he had never asked to receive.

In that moment with Mom on my bunk bed I closed my eyes and saw him from above, a diminishing view of his face as I ascended further and further into the atmosphere, his expression at first defiant, then blank, then kind of scared, framed between my dangling feet, growing smaller and smaller amidst our front-yard stand of sagging, sharp spruce trees until he was a pinprick of light, a flesh dot, and then altogether gone beneath the clouds.

One

I see a universe animated by appetite. All history the story of hunger. For sustenance, shelter, and sex. The hunger for power and love. For fame and gold and vengeance. For a capital G God, or at least some lowercase substitutes.

I see ancient Xerxes war-hungry and on the move, the great Persian Shāhanshāh, king of kings, surrounded by a million, let's say two million soldiers marching west to crush Greece, washing like a murderous wave across the river Maeander. Herodotus said their numbers were so vast that the soldiers not only crossed rivers but drained them with their thirst.

But then Xerxes saw a solitary plane tree on the horizon, majestic and sprawling and mottle-barked, with wide palmate leaves rustling in the breeze. He fell in love with that tree on his way to crush a civilization, and with the lifting of his hand, he screeched his entire war animal to a halt beneath its dappled shade.

I see, then, how hunger cloaked as history stretched westward, setting sunward, Europeans searching for slaves and fame. Devouring. Satiating. Hungry for liberty and space and everything under the whole sky. What, other than raw appetite, could lure so many bodies over a vast, unknown, tempestuous ocean in rickety boats made of cork-oak and pine?

Once ashore, all that appetite scratched and clawed at new earth, a new continent, a spiked horizon of trees.

I heard somewhere that before the North American tree hunger a squirrel could have scampered limb to limb for 728 miles, all the way from the Atlantic to the Mississippi without ever touching the ground. Early explorers ran out of appropriate nomenclature to describe the magnificent tangle. The tree adjectives stalled on their tongues.

The forests only lasted, though, as long as settlers were sufficiently terrified of the immense, damp darkness. Fear only froze them momentarily. It didn't take long for awe and early puritan dread of the woods to turn rapidly to need, to greed, and suddenly the trees—interlaced canopy to canopy, dense jungle from ocean shore carpeting endlessly west, a thick skein of branches and roots and leaves budding, unfurling, needles falling into decay—began to recede.

Tree hunger cut a swathe around each homestead, gnawing at the once 950 million acres of forest for fuel and for space to grow, for raw material to build walls and boats and kitchen tables. Raw material to sate a British Empire ravenous for lumber. Raw material to not die from the cold.

Every burgeoning American industry fed on trees.

Down the eastern seaboard the old-growth pines disappeared. The earth opened. Horses attached to thick-braided hemp ropes yanked over the trunks and tore out the roots. Then the saws got sharper, the arteries for transport wider. Down the eastern seaboard and through the interior hardwood forests of Daniel Boone, clawing for the great longleaf pine belt of the south where 237 billion board feet of timber swayed in the wet breeze, the hunger cut in every direction, inland, stretching further west, always west, great holes opening in the canopies and the dirt turned. Along the Cumberland Plateau settlers ripped out the trees and erected their forts. Trees sharpened into pillars of defense, funneled at their tips into giant piercing spears.

And the cabins. South of Nashville, deep in the valleys, close to water and hunkered down among the curve of rolling hills, a man and woman broke a wooden wagon wheel one day, just passing through, and decided: What the hell, this place looks as good as any other. It was 1797. Johnny "Appleseed" Chapman was concurrently tromping through the Allegheny Mountains sowing apple seeds, one of the few trying to replant, when William and Sarah Nolen staked their claim down south, started yanking hickory and poplar from their roots. They stacked cedar trunks into a cabin, mud between the rounds, carved a space amidst the trees and lived mostly warm, safe, and well fed.

More settlers arrived, more trees toppled. A half-acre in town went for $55, then a hundred, eventually a thousand and then ten more.

The precise Nolensville acres that would someday sustain my family passed from owner to owner like a playing card. The Stovalls, Johnsons, Mayfields—to the Brileys in 1912 under the condition that a fourth of an acre up by the house not be touched, as it was a gravesite, some said, for slaves. The weathered, broken headstones will still be there when we arrive a hundred years after the sale.

But I trace all this history to arrive at a singular seed, a red oak kernel that around 1912 plunged into the soil, adrift from its origin tree, and then ignited, and after rain, after sun, a tiny sapling began to cling to life along a slope that rose from an oval pond, a flickering of thin, silver branches along a small ridge wrapping around water and field. The tree grew. Each year a few inches higher, a few inches thicker. The rings multiplied, each season imprinting the tree's inner flesh with a ring of triumph or challenge. It was all there. A circular, concentric atlas of a life lived. The tree grew and grew—each winter and humid, slippery summer it reached up and out.

And in 1949 the acres passed again, this time to an old army chaplain, one of three captured by the Japanese during World War II and the only one to survive, who finally came home, looked for land and, God bless him, saw the tree.

"A long search ended at the dead end of an un-named road in Nolensville, Tennessee," he writes. "My wife Vi and I spent the next forty years there, most of it trying to restore the place to a livable condition."

His name was Sam Donald. He bought the few hundred acres surrounding the tree and started working endlessly on the old house in the oak's lanky shadow.

It was a good life there. Livable. A kind of delicious freedom.

By the time Sam Donald died there were neighborhoods

eating through the forests around his acres. Tree hunger reshaping the landscape, taking more and more. The farm's new owner posted a For Rent sign down by the road, which had garnered the name of the old chaplain himself.

The tree arched now over the pond, seventy, eighty feet in the air. The old house was empty and cobwebbed. My mom and dad saw the sign during a meandering trip through the countryside: Nolensville farm house for rent: $700, plus utilities.

We had been looking for a place to move Mom's sheep and llamas and goats, a basement to store Dad's paint cans and drop cloths, a field to throw up temporary fencing, occasionally electrified. We were tired. We were transient, having drifted south from upstate New York along the same hunger lines as the old eastern seaboard loggers only to move into a condo in a sea of asphalt.

We found the farm, the tree, the soil, and suddenly felt we could put down some roots.

My big brother and I shared a room in Sam Donald's old house even though we were grown up enough to live on our own. Our sisters down the hall, Amanda and Danielle. Mom and Dad the next door down.

My brother, Aaron, was wild and volatile and mutant strong. I was anxious and inward. Aaron's appetites were mostly physical. Insatiable. Mine centered on something I couldn't quite find the language for. Spiritual, perhaps, although by then I had fallen far away from that five-year-old admission of faith. "Backslidden," my dad said. Lost in a thicket of sin.

Our sisters prayed for our souls and our parents prayed for our souls. My brother and I slept each night with the windows open, regardless of season. We slept in adjacent twin beds to the hum of an oscillating fan and the sound of each other breathing.

We woke each morning with fresh hunger, every morning voracious as hell. Each morning we got up and went together into the trees.

Two

My brother survived high school until the end of his sophomore year and I barely got through freshman. We were good at disappearing. We disappeared from classes and we disappeared from cops. We disappeared from reality on those days we could find the right chemical portals and we disappeared into the canopies of trees. By our late teens we were professional tree climbers. Around the time we could have been sophomores in college we were instead setting ropes in lofty forks and dismantling or deadwooding or pruning our way to paychecks. It was more interesting than algebra. Better paying than painting houses with Dad.

That's how we spent our weekdays: turning trees into money.

On weekends, we hoisted ourselves into the branches of Sam Donald's old oak, eighty feet high now, and sometimes we attached swings and glided out over the little valley because the tree was on that hillside. All we had to do was get a little momentum and suddenly the ground dropped away. We closed our eyes and we were flying.

One weekend we were swinging high and some of the tree crew came over which always made everyone want to go higher. The game was to get on the swing and then someone would grab the frayed tails of rope knotted beneath the swing and run like hell, pulling upward as high as he could before letting go in order to give the biggest and best arc over the little valley, where Mom's sheep and llamas and goats chewed their food and tried to make sense of what was happening above them. These were the gifts we gave each other.

But we couldn't get high enough. And because the boys had come around we started talking about all the ways we could yank that swing heavenward, and then my brother drove the crane truck we used for tree removals out into the field. He parked it beyond the oak and lowered the giant metal arm toward the swing.

Everything made sense in our heads, all the calculations of things that could go wrong and kill someone. Aaron decided he would test it so he went to put on the helmet he sometimes wore when things got dangerous in the trees. One of the boys, the Eagle Scout, hopped over to the crane and worked all the levers. Aaron grabbed the end of the crane arm while he sat on the swing and the Eagle Scout hoisted him fifty feet into the air, almost perpendicular to the ground.

My brother let go of the boom and swung like a pendulum out over the valley and screamed as if he were the kind of bird that screams, a raptor like a hawk or an osprey. He screamed like that the whole way out. It was a beautiful and reckless thing but these things happened to us all the time.

. . .

A fierce wind came through the farm one night and tore the red oak over. The tree fell downhill, toward the pond, and its root flare pulled out of the ground bigger than a dining room table, the broken tendrils jagged and wet.

The next day we grieved over the tree and climbed all over it as it lay there, marveling at all the high limbs, some alive only hours before almost a hundred feet in the air, suddenly crashed to the ground. Some of the branches punctured the ground and drove deep into the soil. We brought out chainsaws and flush-cut the buried limbs. We diced the tree into a million pieces and brought a bulldozer to push them all into a pile. It was a sad and terrible thing. And as the diesel fuel flared and the flames ate the tree we thought about how these things happen to us all the time.

. . .

My brother decided to build a cabin behind Sam Donald's old work-in-progress even though we were just renting. He asked the landlord and received permission, then started milling our towering stack of salvaged oak logs into eight-by-eight beams, and with saws and chisels we created the joints that would dovetail the whole thing together. We hammered in pegs made of locust and the structure started to rise. We might have incorporated the old Sam Donald oak, but a lightning crack had ruined its trunk for milling. It was hollowed out on the inside, which is likely why it fell. Instead, my brother built his house from the trees of our customers' yards, mostly suburban places scattered around town.

We worked in the afternoons, after we returned home from the city with the day's wages. We drank beer as we built, sometimes whisky. We burned scraps of wood in a giant barrel outside the cabin and we stayed up late into the night, sometimes doing pull-ups from the eaves to train for the next state tree climbing competition.

It was coming to Nashville. We were getting ready.

The cabin was twelve feet by twelve feet with a small loft where Aaron put his bed. He ran an extension cord into Mom and Dad's house for a few weeks, then patched a dedicated line right into the grid. He installed switches and a ceiling fan, put a wood burning furnace in a corner and vented it out the wall. He used his crane as a tie-in point and dangled over the cabin with his rope and harness to hammer down a tin roof. Quickly, after only a month or two of tinkering, it was his home.

The days turned cold. Some nights it snowed. We kept the fire going inside, taking the scraps of trees we had dismantled and turning them, piece by piece, into an almost unbearable heat.

In December, on the cusp of Christmas, it was one of those rare Eves when snow was not only falling in Tennessee but actually sticking. The blacktop of the roads vanished and in every corner of the city people were sliding into ditches and telephone poles. Southerners get a little panicked in snow. Like deer caught in headlights, but deer in the driver's seat, the whites of their eyes wide as they go careening off into yards and guardrails.

I yelled this observation to Aaron, who was suspended sixty feet off the ground by a bright, braided rope, pruning his way through a tulip poplar. I was eye level with him in a nearby maple, even though the falling snow was so thick I could barely see him. He grunted acknowledgement and jumped to another limb.

We were on the clock. We were working on Christmas Eve in the middle of a snowstorm because business had been slow and our customer, who was framed in firelight and warmth in his living room below, wanted all his trees pruned before Christmas as a gift to his wife, whose soft silhouette was visible in the room's crackling light.

My brother's body was a blur of motion. I could see his movement through the falling snow, just barely, and he was picking up speed. He was squirrel-like and nimble, jumping from limb to limb and bobbing out on slippery branches to fine prune the tips.

It was so cold. The temperature dropped and our brittle skin cracked and bled. The creases around our knuckles opened and the rough ridges of tree bark punctured our hands. The snow swept over us in white waves and billowed around us like down from a city-wide pillow fight, like all the pillows burst at once and the wind whipped up the white and hurled it around and around.

I was perched in my tree thinking of metaphors for snow. I thought about telling my brother, but I knew the most I'd get from him was a grunt or a string of curses about the cold. Instead I hung quietly in my maple, squinting to see his scratchy wool sweater through the flurry. I could hear his movements, and the biting of his serrated handsaw into the hard flesh of the tree. Every sound seemed amplified by the snow—we were dangling in an acoustic cathedral of white.

All around me I could see the fresh wounds from my pruning and the sap freezing instantly from the cuts into icicles, into tiny stalactites of sugar maple. I yelled "Sapcicles!" to my brother, who was pulling on the cord of his chainsaw to ignite its engine. He severed a dead limb, clipped the saw to his harness and began zipping to the ground, bouncing feet-first off the trunk in graceful arcs. I threw a three-inch shard of frozen sap into the snow at his feet.

Ours was the best job in the world—sometimes. Sapcicles on Christmas Eve in the middle of a snowstorm. No cubicles, no screens. We generated our own warmth by revving the internal engines of our bodies and by running our breath over blood-starved fingertips and by never ever stopping.

I, too, descended to the ground and began unsnapping carabineers and untying knots. I watched as Aaron bent down to pick up the stalactite of sap and I saw the blood stain on the snow from his brittle, broken skin.

"It's fucking cold," he said.

. . .

When we still lived in upstate New York, a year after I said the Sinner's Prayer with Mom, my seven-year-old brother claimed to know every curse word in the world.

He said, "I know how babies are made and how to say the poop word and if you tell on me I'll paint you with black paint and pin you to the road and a truck will come and smash your brains out because he can't see you."

He was poised like a diver on the edge of our bed, preparing to jump into a mound of every piece of clothing and blanket and pillow we could find in our shared room. We lived in Freeville, then, just outside of Ithaca on the eastern edge of the Finger Lakes, and Mom and Dad were members of a Christian commune called Love Inn. We went to school and church in the same old dairy barn—as big and wooden and infused with the divine as Noah's ark. Our teachers spoke in tongues. Our pastors placed their hands on people to heal their bodies and cast out demons. I was freshly born again but never figured out how to speak in tongues or cast out demons. Aaron was growing in his sin. Both of us, though, knew better than to swear.

My brother pretended to jump off a cliff, which was the edge of my bottom bunk, and he planned to say curse words as he jumped because, "That is what you would do," he said.

"Shit!"

He flopped into the soft mound and convulsed as if he were dying, just like in the cartoons we weren't supposed to watch, hanging his tongue out and rolling his eyes into the back of his head. A fish gulping air. He was dead for five seconds before he jumped to his feet and laughed rabid and crazy-eyed, as if he were possessed.

"You can try it too," he said, "but you have to say a curse word on your way down. I will tell you what to say. If you tell Mom or Dad I'll bury you with fire ants and they'll eat your face off and make babies in your skull. Ready? Damn!"

"Damn!"

I fell face-first into the linens, felt the warmth from where my brother's body had just been. I pretended I was dead, too, copying his convulsions before looking to see if I had done it right. He told me to move over because he had a new idea.

"Now I'm on the Empire State Building," he said, crouching on the edge of the top bunk. I told him it was too high, too dangerous. He said he didn't care. "I'm going to jump off in order to kill myself," he said. "You wish you could stop me but you can't because you're on the ground and I'm a million miles on the top of the building. Ready? Fuck!"

The door to our room swung open as my brother face-planted into the clothes and Dad was there with his angry eyes. He walked over to my brother and jerked him up by the arm, then locked his fingers around my arm, too, and dragged us both into the bathroom. He fed us soap and made us swish it around in our mouths and when my brother said, "This tastes like shit!" I was told to leave my dad and brother alone.

...

Aaron and I coiled our ropes and began dragging brush to the mouth of the chipper, which had growled to life. Our chipper could gobble up a section of tree twelve inches thick, giant hydraulic drums tugging the trunk hard against the rotating blades, breaking the forks, spewing shreds of wood into the back of our old GMC. Aaron told me when I first started working with him not to worry, that if I were to get sucked into the mouth of the machine I would go into shock instantly from the trauma. "It would be almost painless," he said, smiling.

This was my brother's company, his universe. He started his business after going AWOL from a previous rag-tag tree company. His old boss had asked him to cut down a tree that didn't deserve cutting down. A magnificent black walnut. A true specimen. It was dropping its green brainy fruit onto the driveway of its homeowners and they were tired of crushing the orbs under their car tires.

"Fuck you, cut it down yourself," Aaron said.

And with that he walked away and put six thousand dollars-worth of saws and tree gear on a credit card, then asked if I wanted to be his ground guy, the brush dragger and rope runner.

"Sure," I said.

He wanted to be a real arborist. A professional tree person. I was simply anxious to earn money for one-way tickets to far off places. I needed a purse to keep me in motion.

That December, after a year of lucrative work, of learning the trade both on and above the ground, I was greasing all the chipper's pivot points in the snow, spinning around to catch a wide, slow-falling flake on my tongue when Aaron hurled a snowball at my face. I recoiled, wiped away the snow and saw that he was already forming more ammunition. "Son of a bitch," I mumbled, staggering behind the chipper for refuge. I felt another snowball glance off my shoulder and heard it explode against the back of the truck. This last one sounded as if there were bits of gravel packed in with the snow. That had always been his method from up north: packed snow around a pit of stone.

"You better wake up quick!" he shouted.

Eleven months apart was enough of an age gap for him to be stronger and faster but close enough for me to be perpetually at his heels. A snowball to the face necessitated swift and severe revenge. There could be no signs of weakness. I scooped up a handful of fresh snow from the top of the chipper and began packing it harder and harder with the heat of my hands. Aaron hopped over some brush staged in the yard and ran to the safety of a tree trunk. I began stalking him. The chipping would have to wait. We had things to settle.

...

We lived on a farm in Freeville, too. Five acres, an 1850s Victorian that was once a six-bedroom inn. It was the first place my parents ever bought and it was the place my mom wanted to live forever. She planted asparagus and carrots and pumpkins. There was a complex of old barns, one where the machines and their implements lived, another where we stored hay and grain for Mom's sheep.

Aaron and I stood in the shadow of the big barn one day, and he said, "I'm huge! I'm a mountain!"

"Which one?" I asked. I had Love Inn geography fresh on my mind. I knew things.

"Mount Kilimanjaro," he said. "It's in Africa, stupid. Or Mount Everest. I'm a giant and I can destroy you."

I fixed my seven-year-old glare onto my eight-year-old brother and pushed my fingers into my arm, into the supple flesh between the humerus and bicep, making a little mound of my skin. A mountain. My muscles were mountains.

"I'm like a Mack truck," I said. "A steamroller and ditch-digger combined. I could roll all over you or dig you up because

I'm metal and gears. I'm the world's biggest transmission and engine plus a flamethrower."

My brother shook his head, laughed, and called me sea sludge, a penny getting run over on a railroad track, squished and flattened. He said he was the train.

"No, I'm big and mean. I'm a thunderstorm and lightning. I'm the implement barn and I'll crush you."

We both looked at the barn. Mt. Kilimanjaro had no real significance. It just sounded big and lived in a textbook with an italicized caption, somewhere in Africa. But the implement barn was *right there*. A true goliath.

And then we noticed the slope of the roof, considered it all, the tin lines running vertically down like tracks and then leveling out like bowling alley lanes.

"I'm a rocket ship," I said. "I'm a fifty-caliber bullet. I could run around you thirty times and you wouldn't even notice because I'm so fast it's scary."

We climbed to the top of the barn and began sliding down.

But the friction. Racing down the tin burned holes in our jeans. So much heat. And we were so small up there, teetering on the spine of that New York barn seeing horses as distant and small as mice and dogwood trees as tiny as bonsai.

"I'm a turbo-powered racecar," I said. "You can try and keep up with me but pretty soon you'll be so far behind you'll cry like a baby. I'm the speed of light, faster than Jesus, faster than the twelve disciples put together."

We had holes in our jeans, but Mom had matching periwinkle blue towels—nice towels from a nice store in the mall, the kind of department store where you could hide in the circular racks of clothes, push aside the slacks, step inside, disappear.

"This towel is my magic carpet and I'm magic," I said. "I'm a big blue genie and I'm putting a spell on you with my speed. You can't even see me because I'm so magic and fast. I kick up magic from my carpet and when you're behind me you eat my magic dust."

We burned through Mom's bath towels and our bellies ached, right in their middles, because we were laughing a deep laugh that was brand new. It took different muscles to laugh like that. We were sore in our very centers.

And then we saw Mom, first a speck in the doorway of the house, backlit from inside, then growing. She came to the edge of the barn and climbed the stepladder thrown up against the roof.

"I'm a mountain," I said. "Lightning, Momma. I'm so fast I could tell you about it but you wouldn't even be able to hear me because my words are so fast only coyotes can hear them."

She was on the roof, then, scooping up the towels, snagging Aaron with one arm and me with the other as I tried to run back up the tin and she spun me around to see the singe marks on the back of my jeans. She had her hand tight around my arm, around my bicep. I was flexing it. Smiling. It felt even more like a mountain under her warm, grasping fingers.

. . .

More than a decade later we called it a draw in our customer's yard. There was snow down my collar and some in my ear and Aaron took one on the cheek. The snow was still falling and the truck was mostly full of wood chips. After an hour of work we had fed all the branches through the chipper and the shards were releasing their last remnants of life and moisture and heat. Steam curled from the chips and crystallized in the cold air. It was beautiful. Everything started to look beautiful in the snow.

Aaron had warmed up the truck's motor and gone to get the check, which we were hoping would cover all of our Christmas expenses and maybe even give us a cushion into January. I was closing in on my next plane ticket, just a few hundred dollars shy. Central Asia, I figured. A one-way ticket. An escape. I saw Aaron in the side mirror pointing out our progress to the customer, who nodded enthusiastically and called his wife over to note the changes. Everyone on the porch was so happy. And when I saw the check change hands, I was happy, too.

My brother surveyed our work as he walked back to the truck and hoisted his compact body into the driver's seat, which he had outfitted with a little cushion to help him see over the steering wheel. He was a small man. The top of his head came just to my chin, yet he was filled with a Napoleonic fire that compelled people to cower or obey. And he had the physical strength to back any order.

He threw the truck into gear and the chipper pulled taut against the hitch and we were off, heading home with our tons of metal and tools and sweet, shredded, steaming bits of tree.

"It's Christmas Eve," he said. "Can you believe it? And a fucking snowstorm."

As we drove home I could see the trees sagging under the weight of snow. I saw the shiny black branches snaking through the passing canopies and then the thick lines of white on top. I pruned all the trees in my mind as we passed at thirty-five miles an hour.

The windshield of the dump truck was smeared and filthy as the oversized wiper blades carried many months of grit— now mixed with snow—back and forth, back and forth across the glass. The heater was cranked so high that we cracked our windows, and the cold air sneaking through cut the humidity seeping from our bodies.

Aaron lit a cigarette and let it hang from his mouth, let the ash fall in his lap as his body bounced with the contours of the road. Everything around us, every smell and sight and sound felt so familiar and good. We knew every strange utterance of the GMC, which Aaron had recently bought with a few months' earnings, and every street was as known to us as our own farm's field, despite the blanket of snow.

We finally wound our way down Sam Donald Road and then we were home. I jumped from the cab to help guide my brother as he backed up the chipper. We connected through the smeared reflection of the rearview mirror. This was one of the few times we actually looked at each other's faces for more than a second or two. His was tanned brown despite the season, and his beard was coming in dark, softening the leathery skin that wrapped tightly around his skull. Everything about him was chiseled. The tips of his shoulder-length hair were bleached from the sun, and his eyes, reflected as they were through the dirty glass of the rearview mirror, were sharp, bright, electric blue.

Looking at his eyes I began miming the universal hand signals for left, a little right, three more feet and a closed fist for *Stop!* His face disappeared from the mirror, the motor died, and Aaron emerged, hopping down into the snow and flicking his cigarette into the burn barrel.

"Good work today," he said. "Probably what tree trimming is like up north."

He swung coils of multi-colored rope over his shoulder and walked heavily to his new cabin. He grabbed a beer from the mini-fridge and threw fresh wood onto the smoldering fire in the pot belly stove.

"I guess we can buy gifts now," I said, remembering too late that Aaron was in perpetual rebellion against family, gift giving, or anything having to do with Jesus Christ.

"Fuck Christmas," he said. "Don't even think about getting me anything."

And I knew he meant it. Aaron had never pulled a punch in his life. He said what he meant and he truly, deeply, without question didn't care about Christmas or its trimmings. I knew he would be much happier gliding through a tree's canopy on Christmas day—bleeding hands curled around the handle of a chainsaw—than sitting stationary beneath a tree covered in ornaments with his family.

...

Love Inn, the Christian commune, was the center of my family's

Upstate universe. Our anchor. And from that center we learned about God and we learned about serving him and when I was eight and Aaron nine, the Ten Commandments were locked securely in our hearts. We could recite them forward and backward by memory, even if the words "adultery" and "idolatry" were awkward and bulky in our mouths. Like swearing, "Thou shall not steal," at least, was crystal clear.

So me sneaking into Mom and Dad's room one early morning, snagging some shiny quarters and dropping them into my pocket was a hell of a deviation, a first foray into the world of outright disobedience, a test for all the sermons of sin and consequence already swimming around in my dreams where they shared real estate with my interpretation of demons—muscled, horned, red-skin on fire. I just wanted to buy a small cardboard round of ice cream from the convenience store down the street, the kind with an attached wooden spoon. I was hungry for something sweet.

But the coins burned. Eleven grams of copper and nickel and sin. I was saved but already producing bad fruit.

And when Dad came howling down the stairs after breakfast, demanding to know who had raided his purse, the full weight of what I'd done filled my body with something like concrete. I hit the floor sobbing, pinned down and heavy with fear. I knew pennies mattered back then. I knew Dad counted every one.

So I confessed. I yelled out my guilt in one long, blubbering confession. Dad shot upstairs to exchange the stolen coins for his Iowa State fraternity paddle, the one Mom had asked him not to use anymore, and suddenly, despite the desperation and sobbing, I felt my brother kneel down and tell me it would be alright. He put his hand on my shoulder and told me that. A nine year-old kid. And when Dad descended my brother stood up and put out his hand as if he were stopping an oncoming train and yelled, "I'll take it for him!"

My father fell silent. Perfectly still. He slowly enunciated my brother's words to make sure he had heard him correctly. "You want to take your brother's spanking?"

"I'll take it for him," Aaron said, pulling out a chair from underneath the table, a chair over which he would have to bend.

"And you?" Dad asked, looking at me with his arched eyebrows. "You'll let your brother take it for you?"

I glanced at Aaron and his face was like stone and I saw the paddle clutched in Dad's hand. "Yes," I said with my eyes on the floor.

Dad then exacted his lesson on my brother's young body, swift smacks of the paddle landing across the backs of Aaron's legs, five, six, seven. I couldn't watch. I turned away. I heard the blows and I heard a kind of muffled crying, sobs pushing against pursed lips, barely audible.

And then silence. The punishment exhausted, only the sound of the chair screeching back beneath the table. I turned to see Aaron walk quickly out of the kitchen, stiff as a board, and I heard him climb the stairs and then slam the door to our room. I wiped away the snot and tears and looked at Dad, who seemed a little stunned, a little sorry.

"Go upstairs," he said quietly, so I obeyed and went to be with my brother.

. . .

Christmas day came and my suspicions about my brother's ambivalence toward the holiday were confirmed. Aaron had gotten a call, a strange request to slice the top off a maple tree in a nearby city. We never did work in this city and we certainly never topped trees. Topping was a response to the urban—and rural!—myth that said if your trees get too tall, they will fall on your house and kill your children as they sleep. The solution, according to the myth, was to simply cut your trees in half, decapitate them, rob them of the opportunity to grow into murderous woody giants that would just as soon send a jagged limb into your bedroom as provide you with shade.

Yet Aaron accepted. We needed the money, yes, so he conveniently forgot every lesson we had ever learned about arboriculture. It was Christmas morning. We were in his cabin, him at his desk and me warming my hands by the stove. Dad knocked at the door.

"What's up?" Aaron said.

Dad opened the screen and sat next to Aaron at the desk. A cup of coffee steamed between his hands.

"Merry Christmas," he said. "You two staying busy?"

"Busy enough," Aaron said. He scribbled a note onto an invoice: *$150 per cable, tree needs three.*

Dad came out every now and again for advice. His painting business had been hit or miss for decades, always in the midst of waxing or waning, and his eldest son, in only a few years, had proven himself a competent, steady, savvy entrepreneur.

"I was thinking of laying off my guys," Dad said. "Can't rely on them, you know? I think I'd do better just getting along by myself. The problem is that it's Christmas and everyone needs the money."

Dad had a habit of hiring vagrants and addicts and people looking for second, third, fourth chances in life. His employees rarely showed up on time, or at all. Sometimes they left with his power sprayers or advances on work they had yet to complete.

"That's stupid," Aaron said without taking his eyes off the invoice. "That's why you're broke all the time. You need to let people make you money."

I looked up and saw Dad, almost sixty, still in his work clothes, a constellation of paint flecks in his thinning hair, a rainbow of stains on his white pants. His lower back was plaguing him again with pain, his once-muscled limbs further atrophied. He dragged buckets up ladders, breathed in all the fumes and ate his lunch from gas station rotisserie stands where he could get hot dogs and taquitos fast and cheap.

"Well, I'll keep that in mind," Dad said, standing up to leave.

"Thanks for the advice."

Aaron waited until the screen door slammed and whispered, "Dumb ass," beneath his breath.

Our family was gathering around the Norway spruce in the living room and divvying up gifts, waiting for us to gather. Dad was there with his tattered leather Bible, the Scofield version, bound and rebound with duct tape, his hands resting on the verses about Christ's birth which had all been marked in highlighter and then underlined in pen. Our sisters were in their pajamas and slippers poking at presents. But Aaron had already been out to warm up the truck.

"You working?" he asked, as if my answer didn't matter.

I was lacing up my boots and pulling on layers and layers of clothing.

"I'm with you," I said.

Aaron yelled into Mom and Dad's house that we would be back in a few hours and we shuffled out to the truck as our parents' protests erupted inside. We hopped in the cab and dragged the chipper out of the long winding driveway and onto the road which, we discovered, had been salted and was now slushy and traffic free. I rubbed my frigid hands together, winced from where the pain pulsed beneath the open cracks, and told my brother how lucky he was to have a worker as good and strong and fast as me.

. . .

My brother's entire life had been bleeding and motion, further and higher. The same fear I felt when I was five, imagining him left behind as I ascended into the clouds, expanded, deepened, then calcified as he took bigger risks.

At fourteen, for example, after we moved down to Tennessee so Dad could find more painting work, Aaron crashed through a car in a marvel of timing and speed that would have made a Hollywood stunt double salivate. The car was cruising along at thirty miles an hour until my brother, running a stop sign on his motorcycle and hitting its side at about forty, brought it forever to a halt. His body flew headfirst in one rear window and out the other, the shrapnel from the broken glass blinding a kid in the backseat. Aaron crumpled onto the street in a pool of blood with quick, heavy breaths hissing through his collapsed lung, and then went into a body cast for six months.

He was held together with titanium rods. Reconstructive surgery on his ruined hands—the skin of which had been peeled back as he crashed through the car—gave him permanent scars. They would never fade.

Mom and Dad sat beside his bed. There was no insurance, no savings. Dad worked eighty hours a week painting Nashville's houses to pay the mounting bills. Mom and Dad cried. They put their hands on their son's body and prayed for healing.

But he wasn't broken. The doctors put him in a wheelchair and, after his release, he learned to pop wheelies through the mall's food court, his stiff, plastered legs bobbing above the tables, all the mothers gasping. His friends would visit him at home and scribble anarchy symbols and penises on the plaster cast wrapped around his body.

Destruction seemed to follow him everywhere. It was his wake.

A South Carolina beach, a rare family vacation, he was allowed to bring his friend Thomas along for the week. They prowled the beach each day, chasing the few girls they could find and torturing any beach life they could catch. The sand crabs had it the worst. Aaron and Thomas trapped the things two at a time and held cans of bug spray over their wiggling bodies, spraying their shells until they glistened with toxicity.

Then the matches, the flick, the flame. After the release the crabs had a few seconds of scampering before the fire cooked them alive inside their shells. Aaron and Thomas shrieked victory or defeat accordingly and ran off to find more victims. It happened over and over again. Their appetite for torture was so ravenous it quickly jumped from sand crabs to me, little brother, a perfect target every time I wandered out of Mom and Dad's earshot.

Their favorite method was Big T, or "Big Torture," which was Aaron's version of Chinese water torture, a technique he saw on a television documentary once.

"The forehead is the ideal place," he said. "It takes a while, but the victim eventually goes crazy with the drip. Enough time and the drops of water turn into fists and each one feels like you're getting hit in the face."

I got it in the chest. Aaron held, Thomas thumped. My tears didn't matter, my threats were met with harder *thwaps*. Only after they both got bored would they finally fling themselves away. I would touch my chest to see if they had broken the skin.

Sometimes I imagined the list of my brother's sins as muscled roots going deep within the earth, the heavenly pull of the rapture unable to yank him from the ground, no matter how much Jesus might have wanted to.

By sixteen my brother seemed indestructible. His friends had started calling him "The Mutant." It was his forearms. Gigantic and veiny, like a cow's udder except rock solid. The fact that his body sort of faded from the shoulder blades down added to the effect. He was all neck and shoulder and gorilla arms.

He bolted from Nashville before his seventeenth birthday, headed west for Yellowstone and got a job as a dishwasher in a lodge. He made lots of friends, slept with some dreadlocked girls, and backed slowly away from grizzlies and elk, wisely avoiding eye contact.

He was living a specific fantasy that had become popular in our pocket of Tennessee, a *head west young man* vision laced with lots of psychedelic drugs. They all grew out their hair, traded bootlegged Grateful Dead tapes and bought foreign pick-up trucks, talking incessantly about community and simple living and the disease of materialism.

Many headed west to perform menial jobs in ideal settings.

California, Colorado, Montana. Snowboard bums and house-cleaners, surfers and construction workers. There was sex and rock and roll and a constant hunger for a deeper bigger better high. My brother fit right in.

When I spent my entire savings to fly out and visit him at sixteen, I found him living in the back of his Nissan 4x4 in an empty parking lot in Crested Butte. He had rigged up the truck bed into a remarkable little cubbyhole of efficiency, with racks for his pots and pans, Tupperware containers for all his belongings and a passenger floorboard for all of his crumpled cans of beer.

We fell asleep side by side that first night after cooking black beans over his camp stove. Conversation lurched along for the next few days as if our words were vehicles working out their position in rush hour traffic. Stop and go, change lanes, honk and give each other the finger. We weren't used to having so much space and time to talk. We reminisced about some things, fantasized a little about the future, talked a lot about Mom and Dad and then decided to drive to Oregon to see the Grateful Dead.

The Dead were playing one of their rare modern shows where fans could camp in the parking lot. More a makeshift, impermanent carnival than a concert. And for us, it was a weekend of hallucinations and dancing and adrenaline. Neither of us invited Jesus along for the ride.

There are times when one's body feels like it can't contain the high, when the joy and beauty and electricity of it all turns into something like ache, something almost sacred. And I think that's what we felt. At least that's what *I* felt. We hit Idaho on the way back with heads full of mescaline and I felt like I would rather be out there on the road with my brother than anywhere else in the world. I never told him that. But I think he knew. I think he felt the same.

...

We reached our Christmas jobsite and surveyed the project. Aaron talked to the customer, explaining again the detrimental effects of topping trees, but the homeowner insisted he had a double-wide and children to protect, and dammit if he was going to allow some maple tree to come along and ruin everything. Aaron shrugged and snapped into action, cranking the leather straps of his spikes tight around his calves and rotating his ankle to get the slender steel bridge resting properly in the arch of his foot. He scampered up the trunk and, in a frenzy of gas-powered noise and sailing wood chips, began slicing away the top of the tree.

Such indiscriminate cutting made the job go quickly. Suddenly the maple was topless. It looked cartoonish, grotesque. And because we had lopped off its branches, taking away the tree's ability to photosynthesize in a matter of minutes, it would soon go into shock and, in an attempt to survive, thrust up a thousand water sprouts from the severed ends of its limbs. The water sprouts would be weakly attached and much more dangerous than the tree's original structure. In three years the tree would be a far greater liability than it was that morning.

We tried. Some people simply won't listen. I dragged the brush to the chipper as my brother packed up his gear, and soon all the limbs were chipped and piled, steaming, into the back of our truck, and we were on our way home with a bigger cushion to usher us into January. My brother's predictable cigarette dangled from his cracked lips and he squinted into the sun. His vise-like, battered hands at rest, one riding the steering wheel and the other curled loosely around the shifter, buzzing against the plastic.

...

When my brother finally returned from his adventures out

west he wanted simply to pass through Tennessee on his way to wherever. He wanted to explore the east for a while, perhaps the veins of white water splashing through North Carolina and Virginia.

But his tire blew when he reached Nashville. His tire blew and he had no money to replace it and just like William and Sarah Nolen he decided what the hell, might as well stick around for a bit. He surfed couches and looked for odd jobs and eventually discovered that swinging through trees with a chainsaw attached to a rope could be lucrative. And he was built for it—physically, psychologically. He was a prodigy climber and fearless. Before long he had left his first boss, started his own company, constructed his cabin and bought his equipment and hired me as his helper on the ground. Then we set about the business of almost dying all the time.

I remember that one hackberry, for example, a tree as big as a house. Tennessee hackberry has this gray, gritty flesh that looks like muscle, all gnarled and callused. And Aaron was taking the giant tree down piece by piece with his crane. He was attached to the tree itself, his rope running through a high limb he could use as a vantage point to work through the entire canopy. The crane was for removing each section, but each section was a thousand pounds of bone-crushing weight, dripping out its life, wrapped up with a sling attached to a cable running into the guts of the crane. So many carabineers and ropes and pulleys. Hydraulic fluid pumping through hoses and moving the mechanical arm—a fifty foot reach—through the air and the Eagle Scout was at the helm, as he usually was, working all the knobs and levers like a kid in control of a giant toy. Aaron was shouting directions from the top of the hackberry. It was his life up there. An inch was life or death in this business, a lost leg or a substantial paycheck.

"Fuck, Jesse, left!" he screamed, and the Eagle Scout nudged the boom an inch left.

Then Aaron pulled up the big chainsaw because he was

down to the big wood, wood as thick around as a table top, and he was taking the hackberry down in four foot sections, slicing first a wedge, then a back cut, and then the sections fell just right, the sling cinched like a noose, and the Eagle Scout hoisted the pieces safely to the ground, where I waited with a rake.

A thousand pounds of hackberry would crush my brother flat, especially if it had a little momentum. And he knew it. So he was doing everything methodically, and screaming at Jesse, "Fuck, Jesse, right!" and the Eagle Scout obeyed with his palm on the lever, he nudged right, but just that once he got the angle slightly wrong, an inch wrong, and the section of hackberry pivoted on its holding wood, then swung around under the crane's boom and headed straight for my brother's head. I was watching. I was wringing my knuckles around my rake and watching. The wood came for my brother in a swift, deliberate swing, and at the exact second he was about to get flattened he let go of the trunk, surrendering himself to his rope and harness, and thrust his boots against the rushing wood, riding the piece of hackberry into the sky, riding out its force until it exhausted its arc, and then he swung gently back to the trunk where he stuck as if magnetized to the gray.

I saw the Eagle Scout, whose face had gone chalk white. I squinted up at my brother's silhouette, a small dark mass dangling fifty feet up the skeleton of a half-gone hackberry.

"I said right, Jesse," he said, and from his perch my brother calmly started untying knots and rearranging slings, readying himself to remove the next section of tree.

. . .

We were almost home, winding our way along back roads that felt as if they belonged only to us. Everyone else, the whole family, the whole world, it seemed, was curled up in living rooms with mountains of wrapping paper piling at their fuzzy-slippered feet, Christmas lights pulsing.

But I was happy to be with my brother. To be in motion with him. We hadn't said anything for miles and, maybe because it was Christmas day and we had been silent for a while, I thought of the story of Zacchaeus, the small-statured Bible character who climbed a tree to get a better look at the Messiah. Our New York Love Inn teachers told us all about him, made his cut-out likeness on a felt board, bearded, sandaled, and robed. We all sang the song:

Zacchaeus was a wee little man,
and a wee little man was he.
He climbed up in a sycamore tree
For the Lord he wanted to see.

According to the gospels, which I hadn't read in years, Jesus was below in tree shade, surrounded by a large, healing-hungry crowd grabbing at the hem of his garment, desperate for even his shadow to pass over them. But Zacchaeus wasn't so bold. He was a bad man, riff raff, a tax collector who knew he was so unclean that a genuine son of God wouldn't even get close to him.

And when the Savior passed that way
He looked up in the tree.
And said, Zacchaeus, you come down!
For I'm going to your house today!

I considered making a joke out of it, telling my brother how he reminded me of a short little tree-climbing Bible character, and how Jesus walked right up to Zacchaeus in his sycamore, a *Ficus sycomorus,* close kin to Xerxes' locus of worship, and asked him for a place to stay. Imagine how it would feel to have Jesus zero in on you in the midst of that whole crowd, I wanted to say.

Zacchaeus was a very little man,
But a happy man was he,
For he had seen the Lord that day
And a happy man was he;
And a very happy man was he.

"Do you ever feel like you're searching for something?" I asked. Aaron glanced at me, smirked, then went back to scanning the road through the cracked windshield. He was used to my existential probing of everything.

I stared out the window, too, and imagined Jesus standing at the base of one of my brother's trees, looking up through the severed branches into Aaron's fiery blue eyes. I imagined Jesus saying, *Hurry down, Aaron, I need to stay in your house today.* And as my brother descends, bouncing in swift arcs to the ground, I imagined a new look on his face, one I had never seen before. The winter-worn leathery lines were still there, the powerful jaw and muscled neck, but as he reached the ground I saw him exhausted for the first time, frail. He stood before the messiah and slumped over, finally broken.

"Why do you climb?" I asked.

"Because I'm good at it," he said with a laugh. "It makes me happy."

I imagined the Jesus I once thought I knew folding my small brother into his arms, putting his calloused carpenter hands—pierced through—on the back of Aaron's head and pulling his face into all the flowing robes and light.

"Do you still feel strong?" I asked as he threw the truck into first and began the long climb up Sam Donald's driveway.

"I feel stronger than I've ever been," he said, his voice barely audible above the truck noise and engine rumble, his reconstructed hand guiding the GMC home like a ship captain's on a sea-smooth wooden helm.

Three

Winter that year eventually released its grip, as it always does, and summer snuck quickly in. With the heat also came a cyclical spike in cicadas. If you lay on your back in Sam Donald's field, stared straight up at the sky, the insects would crisscross your vision like buzzing paper airplanes. The air throbbed. You could feel the love-hungry hum all through your body.

Mom and I were in the field among the cicadas. We were half-hidden by grass and there was a dead rabbit at her side. She was stroking its white fur even though there was no life beneath it.

"The coyotes chased it last night and trapped it behind the barn door," she said. "Its heart must have been beating so fast it seized up."

"Faster than a hummingbird's wings," I said. "Poor thing. Scared to death."

The coyotes were perpetually rabid, sometimes successful in their hunting, and I dug all the graves around there. When I could find the remains. I filled our rented soil with carcass so Mom wouldn't have to because she hated death more than anything. I took the job seriously, too. I searched for headstones on the hill and only stopped when I found one that looked like it would properly fit the animal being buried. Cursed the predators. Dug deep.

I was good with a shovel because I climbed trees and I planted them too. I knew this from the business: "dig a hundred-dollar hole for a fifty-dollar tree." The same ethic applied to Mom's burials. I made a wide circle with my shovel and scraped off the sod, placing it in a separate pile, then worked my way around and around until I had a nice deep hole, deep enough that the coyotes couldn't smell the death, which would get them digging, too.

It happened. I was away once when Mom tried to bury Valentine by herself, her ancient chocolate-colored sheep, but she misjudged the depth, couldn't lift the ewe back out of the grave, and finished off the hole with only an inch or two of dirt. The coyotes were digging and ravenous by dusk. Mom wheel-barrowed out wood chips borrowed from my brother and spread them over Valentine, then tacked a tarp over that, but the coyotes still came. Then the vultures. Mom went inside and turned up the TV and wept into her palms.

That's why I dug the graves around there. A hundred-dollar hole for a fifty-dollar tree. I put boxwood twigs in the grave, too, not because they had any real significance, but I liked boxwood and so did Mom. And I figured all our ceremonies start that way. We make something up—a handful of dirt on a casket, a slug of liquor poured onto concrete—call it sacred, repeat it over and over and suddenly we have ceremony.

Boxwood was ours. I finished the grave, stood over the dark Tennessee dirt, let my sweat fall. We walked back to the pond and Mom called the turtles to her. She had a magic. She beckoned the turtles and their dark, diamond-scored shells surfaced on the water. They started to drift toward the edge where we sat, their tiny nostrils flaring. They loved my mom.

So did all the animals milling around, the llamas that wandered over, lowering their long faces to the back of her head, breathing in her smell. The wild goose and gander that lived for her touch, running their silky white necks under her hands. Every cat and dog and sheep and goat was love-sick for her, which is why she spent most of her days out there in the field. When things up at the house got complicated the field stayed simple enough. She could come out and yell "Sheep!" and just the name of their species got them running up so quick it was like she was their long lost queen.

As we sat by the pond she said, "I got a call the other day from my friend Merle in Knoxville, the one with all the cows."

She was speaking slow and deliberate. We had nowhere else to go, nowhere we'd rather be.

"Merle said he caught the tail end of that big storm that came through last week," she said. "He was scared for his cattle but the rain and lightning were so bad he had to wait till morning to check on them. He had to search around for a while. They had all gathered under a tree in a little holler. All of them were there."

She paused, thread a piece of grass through her fingers. The cicadas were a symphony.

"Lightning had struck the tree and killed them all," she said quietly. "They were all slumped together at the base of the tree."

I pictured the farmer standing there, calculating his loss, the misfortune, working through the logistics of carting away so many carcasses—the size of the graves and the energy it would demand to dig them all by hand.

"He started winching them into a trailer," she said. "He and some of his friends, but when he winched this one heifer, a baby calf shot up from underneath, from where it had been smothered, and landed on wobbly feet and just stared at the men."

Mom had a far off look on her face, painting the wavy humid air around us with her story, moving Merle and his friends around us like puppets on story-strings. She was gifted in the telling.

"Merle said the calf stood there for a few more seconds kind of googly-eyed," she said, "and then just jumped up a hundred and eighty degrees and bolted, jumped over the barbwire fence and ran straight toward—get this—Knoxville. Merle and his friends searched for it all day but couldn't find a trace. No one's seen it since. "

Mom laughed. Then I laughed too. This was her eulogy, the story of Merle's calf shaking off the storm's electricity, giving death the finger, staring death straight in the face and saying, *Go back to hell, death, I'm not going to die—I'm going to hop this fence and paint Knoxville electric fucking red.*

Mom gave our heart-broken rabbit to the ground with a proper meditation on life.

...

Mom met Dad when he was beating the hell out of his drums for Jesus at Love Inn. He was one of the elders there, a church that met in a barn donated by a widow. Before Love Inn became the center of my family's life, though, it was a hub for the charismatic, hyper-evangelical washouts of the late sixties and early seventies. Young people who had followed a hippy-looking messiah straight out of the drugs and chaos of the Age of Aquarius. They were saved. They wanted to go save everyone else, too.

Dad lived there, drumming with his eyes closed and his head bobbing back and forth like a buoy caught in a strong tide. The Holy Spirit was with him, in him, working through him, he liked to say. He knew because of his audience, who would sob and worship and repent of their sins.

"They would wave their hands and people were healed," he said. "People fell on the ground. I was calling down God's kingdom, on earth as it is in heaven."

My dad's dark, kinky hair encased his head like a motorcycle helmet. He wore leather bellbottoms made by the same tailor who constructed all of Janice Joplin's clothes. But he left that Haight-Ashbury scene, got himself born again and moved to upstate New York where he joined a radical community conspicuous even among a whole generation of radical communities. The Love Inn folks were on *extra*-fire. There was no lukewarm there. Lukewarm got you spit out of the Lord's mouth like gum that had lost its flavor.

Then Dad met Mom, who walked into the sanctuary one day, trapped all the stained glass light in her hair and palpitated his heart as if he had just *thwapped* the living hell out of his snare drum.

"Welcome to Love Inn," he said. "I can show you around if you'd like."

He was desperate for her to say yes. She said yes.

"We share everything here," he said. "God takes care of us.

Of all our needs."

My mom took the tour but wasn't too excited about my dad. He seemed so sure of himself, zealous and overbearing. He was pushy about his God and Mom felt fragile. She said she felt two dimensional back then. Flat. Out of focus.

It started at school, at the tiny Christian college where she first understood she was pretty, understood because a visiting Bible professor gave her verses to memorize and then invited her out to dinner.

"You're a beautiful young woman," he said.

A dinner turned into an invitation to come nanny for his children. Mom said she should have known better, should have understood that wolves can sound just like doves, and that sin can fester just beneath a layer of silk tie, tweed jacket, and feigned piety.

"You're a beautiful young woman," he said again in the kitchen at midnight, his pants around his ankles, his wife and children asleep upstairs. Mom stood backlit against the open refrigerator holding a carton of milk to her chest, a cardboard shield of skim, feeling something click inside. A kind of turning off. A sudden numbness.

She traveled to Love Inn because she had heard rumors that there was something happening in that old dairy barn in Upstate. Demons coming out of people. The Holy Spirit coming in. Rumors of people's infirmities healed, rumors of happiness, a kind of happiness that transcended even those scenes from Woodstock and San Francisco. She took a weekend and caught a ride with a friend and walked into the barn only to meet my father.

My father the elder was also a full-time member of the Phil Keaggy Band—the bell-bottomed foursome named for the nine-fingered virtuoso considered "The best guitarist in the world" by either Eric Clapton, Jimi Hendrix or Eddie Van Halen, depending on who was telling the story. My dad was the rhythm-keeper—eyes closed, head swaying—keeping the best guitarist in the world in time. He was pretty good, too. Not the best, but one of the few drummers who could claim both an intimacy with God and the ability to really jam, to take the churning, ever-evolving sound of early seventies music to a new level.

"A higher level," he said to Mom as he wrapped up his tour. "We're seeking excellence because our God is excellent. Only the very best for Him."

She was so beautiful. He wanted her. And then he heard, quite literally, God telling him that she would be his. He said the voice came from the rafters. It was thrumming through the air. How could he argue with the whisper of God in his hungry ear?

It took a while. It took a year for the two to finally become one. Dad sent long, theologically-charged love letters to Mom, who read them with disinterest until one day she returned to Love Inn and was surrounded by the elders who lay their hands on her and asked for the Holy Spirit to come, to open her eyes to the calling of the Lord, who seemed hell bent on getting her hitched to God's drumming zealot, my skinny, Jesus-eyed dad.

The Spirit came. Mom felt it, she said, and then felt a brand new language begin flowing from her stomach, words she'd never formed, strange sentences that might have been gibberish if it weren't for the reactions of the elders. She was communicating. The elders were more fervent with each word, egging her on: "Yes, that's it," they said. "That's the Holy Spirit so just let it come, keep speaking, keep speaking. Use more B's and L's."

She lifted up her hands in the middle of that circle and stared up at the rafters of the barn and spoke in a new language to a God who had just miraculously fiddled with life's reception knob and turned her vision back from two-dimensional to three.

Dad got the phone call on the road, heard that this love of his had been born again and was waiting for him to return.

"She is transformed, Terry," said a brother into the receiver. "It's just night and day. You've got to get back here."

He returned. Prayers were electric between them, the spiritual connection palpable. They stayed up all night talking and reading scripture and fantasizing about how they might be used by the Lord, how their family might be used by the Lord. That's a reference to me, my brother and sisters—The Family. The young dairy farmer's daughter from Upstate, although she didn't realize it, was about to simply become Mom.

...

After my brother and I would wake up and go into the trees my dad would leave our Sam Donald farm every day in his paint truck, a sagging Dodge minivan gorged on equipment and drop cloths and buckets of spackle and color. He had practiced faux finish techniques to make walls look like marble or clouds or camouflage. He realized he could make double or triple what he would normally earn by posturing himself as a "faux finish artist." Any redneck could paint a room. Only an artist could make your walls look like a checkerboard or a grove of deciduous trees.

And so every day he left the farm and entered the fumes. He came home late in the afternoons and parked the van in the gravel driveway and cranked up evangelical preachers or experimental jazz. Sometimes Dad sat out there for an hour, sometimes more. Sometimes I would come out and find him asleep and snoring with the CD on repeat, an open can of beer wedged between his legs, half empty. I would open the door and the smell of paint and chemicals and sweat would pour out of the van like a palpable fog.

"Long day?" I'd ask.

He'd yawn, stretch, remember the beer and pull it to his lips. "Yeah, long day."

The summer deepened the year the rabbit died. It was epically hot. The days grew longer and the afternoon sun cast long shadows. Nighttime on the farm bristled with heat and life and death.

Always, the circling coyotes.

But one night Mom stirred in bed by the open window, Dad snoring quietly beside her, and she listened past his breathing to the ewe down at the barn, bleating. It was no dream. She leapt from bed before her eyes adjusted to the darkness and lunged for the field, blindly, knowing each step by heart. She reached the barn and saw the stillborn lamb breathless at its mother's feet, weeks too early, the ewe nudging the limp little body with her nose and the rest of the sheep gathered around to look.

Mom was furious now, unwilling to lose another from her flock, so she pulled the lamb's face to hers, waited for a breath, found none, breathed into the sticky open mouth but the lamb's lungs didn't catch the air. Her anger grew so she took the lamb by its skinny ankles and began swinging it around, spinning on her heels, a motion perfected in a thousand airplane games with her children, while the ewe and the others backed away in confusion.

She was lost in her anger because she hated death more than anything and she swung the baby in a wide circle around her body until suddenly the lamb sucked some breath into its lungs and lurched, a blast of electricity in the blood. Mom slowed her spin and placed the lamb on its four impossibly thin legs and it stood.

. . .

Dad quit drumming after I was born. It was too much to stay on tour, too much to juggle; all that ministry and two little boys at home. Then a sister! Tiny and indestructible and gurgling Amanda. A family of five, all with hungry bellies and wild eyes. Especially Aaron's. As soon as Aaron could sit up—his silky blond hair rocketing from his scalp and dribble collecting in a pool in his lap—he ignited a full-on battle of wills with Dad.

"Listen here, old man," he said. "I may look small but I'm not going to take any shit from you. And about all this spiritual nonsense and drumming. Grow up, man. Get a real job and take care of your family."

Or something like that.

Strangely enough, Dad had ears to hear. He traded in his drum sticks for stir sticks and launched what would become four decades of house painting and wallpapering.

Love Inn was changing, too. The elders were part of an apostolic movement led by some big name, big personality Christians who, according to Dad, were getting heavy-handed when it came to discipleship. Spiritual mentors were asking their acolytes to mow their lawns on the weekend. People in leadership took the concept of shepherding so dictatorially that Dad, one of the elders, felt like his freedoms were getting swallowed up by a pharisaical version of Christianity. Drums had faded out of his life almost completely, replaced with endless days of rolling and spraying. And some of his brothers and sisters in the Lord, he felt, had become even worse than the exploitative, egomaniacal gurus of Haight-Ashbury. Dad was eventually called a liability and asked to lay down his eldership.

And what does one do when a community ejects you? In Dad's case one moves. One moves the family in a giant yellow Ryder truck full of all the antiques and animals one can fit in the back and in the cab. One moves to the South and keeps painting, seventy, eighty hours a week to pay for the mortgage on a condo, a condo in the middle of a row of condos, the first place one's family has ever lived with central heat and air conditioning. One finds a church, tiny Bethel Chapel that declares: *We are the single group of believers in this town where the Holy Spirit of God is manifest. We can prove it with our tongues, with the miracles that sizzle through our sanctuary on Sunday mornings.* One writes a play, anything to keep a creative outlet open, calls it *Small World Big Kingdom,* and casts one's ten-year-old son, Josh, in the lead role. One's son, Josh, is told that he is an instrument of God. Anointed. Anointing oil ran into the beard of Aaron, the brother of Moses, says the Bible, and Josh's brother Aaron has joined a Nashville gang called The Daggers and Aaron is using his young body to sleep with girls and fistfight boys and he is sucking smoke and whiskey into his young body. Whiskey is pouring down Aaron's chin like anointing oil down Aaron's chin and the family hungers for a solid rock on which to stand.

...

Metropolitan Nashville in the early nineties couldn't have been more different than our rural Freeville, New York of the eighties. It was a southern city reaching hard for the cosmopolitan. The music industry pulled in so many beautiful people. The publishing industry, too. And so the churches on Sunday morning were almost indistinguishable from awards ceremonies. It was the Grammies every Sunday. The stars came out to connect to God spiritually and network professionally. Everyone was so dashing. There wasn't a city on earth where Sunday morning worship was so impeccably played. Every worship leader did double duty in music studios—Sunday at church and Monday back on the road with Vince Gill.

Dad couldn't hang with the studio guys. He never learned how to read music, just how to *feel* it. But the music-reading studio guys could feel it, too. Dad was an incomplete package. What he was good at, what made him stand out in a city over-populated with shining stars, was his painting.

He made little calling cards that said: "Faux Genius"—his name, his number, the tiny illustration of a painter squinting at his outstretched thumb, making sure the job was done right.

Dad would drum on an old kit in the basement of Sam Donald's house, rattling the walls, the pots and pans. He would stay down there for hours punishing the toms and cymbals, trying to get the paradiddles just right, running through a rhythm over and over until it felt perfect. When he finished he would climb from the basement and get on the phone and set up his paint jobs for the next day, then flop down in front of the television where he would eventually fall asleep. The night preachers would emerge on the Christian station and scream their apocalyptic lullabies.

One morning in the summer of cicadas Mom woke up and went out to her animals and Dad got ready for work as he always did and drove the overburdened minivan to a bid. It was a big job, a few thousand square feet of faux finish interior work. His customer was a woman who begged her husband to hire Dad because he was a real artist, not just some hillbilly painter.

The job seemed to last and last. Dad forgot a brush one day and had to go back to retrieve it. The next day it was a dropcloth. The days got longer and hotter and he kept coming home deeper in evening shadows.

One day I heard Dad talking hushed and strange on the phone at his desk. It looked like he was giggling.

"Who's that?" I asked.

"My buddy," he said, getting up from his desk and walking quickly past me.

I followed him outside. He went straight for the minivan, swung open the rear door and started fumbling through his tools, organizing things and reorganizing them, folding a crumpled drop cloth and stacking scattered swatches of color.

"Who's your buddy?" I asked.

"That's none of your business."

He slammed the tailgate and walked back to the house where he slumped in front of the TV and rummaged in the bottom of a bag of microwave popcorn, looking for unpopped kernels, his fingertips slathered in artificial butter and salt.

Later that night he wrote me a short letter explaining how he might have allowed a certain friendship with a customer to cross a few lines. Then Mom went poking around the computer the next day and saw the fresh document, *lettertoson.doc*, sitting conspicuously in a desktop folder.

Mom read the letter and her heart cracked open. She wandered outside, then drove around the field on the riding mower, full throttle for an hour, crisscrossing through the tall grass until the machine finally ran out of gas. The field dust filled her lungs and the cut grass went airborne then settled on her wet skin, a thatch of brown and green.

Four

Aaron and I had been training for the next state tree climbing championship. It would be held in Nashville, only a twenty-minute drive from Sam Donald's house. We imagined our friends there. We imagined cameras flashing. We started racing each other around our customers' trees during the day, climbing more at home once we returned. We were strong. We taunted each other with accusations of weakness, softness. I had been having dreams where I would do pull-ups, one after another, sometimes one-armed without getting winded. I woke up each morning and did twenty real pull-ups before getting ready for work, which was eight to twelve hours of dragging my body weight up endless vertical feet, fighting gravity, mostly winning, day after day.

Tree climbing competitions in those years were the codification of hubris, the same energy we harnessed every day on our job sites to do impossible things shaped into timed and judged events. It started back in 1976, the year I was born, all that trash talking and ribbing made official. "Tree Trimmer's Jamboree," they called it, which quickly evolved into events that mimicked the new techniques of the industry. The "Foot Lock," the "Body Thrust," a "Throwline" challenge that simulated the method we used to set ropes in the highest and best forks.

Those old climbers simply put a bell at forty feet and timed each other as they scrambled to reach the top. They marked off those choice forks with tape and devised a point system for nailing them with a throwline. They even hoisted a giant dummy up a tree—a crude representation of a climber electrocuted by a power line or knocked out from a removal-gone-wrong—and challenged contestants to get the hell up there and rescue him.

The whole thing took off. It was a weird sport, fun to watch. It was the stuff we did every day but now with spectators and prizes and when we flexed, which we did all the time anyway, a whole audience was there to cheer. To notice. Moms and dads, girlfriends and cousins. Perhaps even the local news or tertiary ESPN.

Aaron took third place the first year he competed for the Tennessee championship. It was the throwline event that robbed him of first. His climbing was magnificent, transcendent, but he kept throwing his line everywhere except the marked forks. Sometimes straight in front of him with a long, reaching bend, once backwards into a crowd of spectators.

"Headache!" he screamed as the fourteen-ounce bag plummeted into a circle of his friends and family. With an allotted five minutes to secure up to three ropes through designated forks, he failed to set even one.

This year would be different. This year I was competing for the first time, having only in the last few years conquered my fear of heights. I had been so sick of dragging brush and feeding the chipper on the ground that I asked Aaron if he would teach me, despite my nauseating fear of being up high. One day he tied my knots and showed me how to ascend and told me to get up a smooth-barked sycamore in order to chase down all the dead branches. Anthracnose fungi had been feasting. Sunken cankers pockmarked all the twigs. The tree was in decline, being slowly eaten away.

I hoisted my body thirty feet into the air and froze. My legs were visibly shaking. I couldn't let go of the trunk. Couldn't even look at the ground.

"You'll be fine," Aaron yelled. "Just move."

I couldn't move. So my brother tied a pole saw onto the bottom of the rope and gave me something to do.

"Pull this up and see what you can reach from where you're at," he said.

I was able to look down, then slowly yank up the pole saw, which clanked against the trunk as it rose. When I had pulled it all the way to my harness, I clipped it to a carabineer and looked around the tree's canopy, which was broad and deep. Mottled white bark and giant green foliage, like a frog's webbed feet. It was Xerxe's ancient tree manifest in modern Nashville. I could see slivers of dark gray dead branches all around, some at the very tips of long, horizontal limbs.

"You'll be fine," said my brother. "Just move a little."

I started swiping at what I could reach with the pole saw, timidly stretching from my position against the trunk. I actually stepped out onto a limb, just a little, using my tie-in point above for leverage. I could see where I wanted to go, just another three feet out where I could reach a few pieces of deadwood on limbs both above and below.

"You trust these ropes?" I yelled, over-gripping the half-inch braid above me, pulled taut with my weight.

"Every day," Aaron said. "That thing could hold fifty of you."

I moved cautiously through the canopy, sawing what deadwood I could safely reach, swatting at the rest, eventually moving up to another tier of limbs, then to the very crown. I remember stopping for a full minute at the top, the green hills of Nashville seemingly at my feet, feeding on the view not *of* the tree like Xerxes, but *from* its highest forks. I felt newly alive. A swell of satiety. I was strong, healthy, engrossed in meaningful work. I was higher than I had ever hoisted myself before. I was freshly in love with a job and what it afforded me, in love with my city and leaving my city, the smells of chainsaw gas and cut wood and the new scent of a friction knot's burning synthetic fibers screaming down a braided line. I was hovering at a height I never imagined reaching on my own. For a moment I felt a tiny suspension of the hunger that turns every cosmic gear—alone in the tops of a tree being eaten from within.

The next day's climb was easier, and the day after. A week of ascension and, suddenly, moving through a tree felt almost like moving along the ground. The distance between had shrunk, and then seemed to altogether disappear.

It wasn't long before I was training for the Tennessee championship. Not to win, but just to do it, and to do it with my brother. I was content to be the underdog, the upstart who learned the trade quickly, and who was now chasing the state title in under a year.

This year's competition was held at a botanical gardens close to town, a sprawling 55 acre campus full of specimen trees freshly pruned for our events. We were giddy and electric. We were eager and wiry. We had been strategizing, practicing for each event. I had a special idea for the aerial rescue, one that I had been dreaming up for weeks. I'd been envisioning the 170-pound dummy—made heavy with Corn Flakes—cradled safely in my arms, lowered peacefully to the ground.

Aaron, who was currently the state's fastest climber in both the foot-lock and body-thrust ascension events, had been demolishing all of us at work. He was, as always, the one to beat.

...

When I was a kid, long before I went into the trees, I wanted to be either the guy who drove the ditch digger down the street from my house—the one that could chew giant holes into the ground—or a break-dancer. I practiced both, just to keep my options open. I worked the levers on my all-metal, authentic replica ditch digger bought from the co-op by my father, who bounced a check to get it for me. And I went to the theatre to see my favorite break-dancing movie, *Breakin'*, over and over again because I told my parents it was just a harmless dance movie, and I slurped up caffeine throughout the film only to rush home and practice the moves in my bedroom to Michael Jackson's *Thriller*, which I wasn't supposed to listen to or watch, but I had seen the whole video at a friend's house and taped the song directly from the radio in secret.

It was another rebellion, I guess. A surreptitious sin. I was slipping further away from the light.

But I had such moves, like the one where I'd jump one-eighty off the bed holding an invisible microphone to my mouth just as Jackson sang: "You hear the door slam and realize there's nowhere else to run."

Then, because I'd be in my green socks with the yellow rings at the calves, I'd slide to one end of the hardwood and moonwalk my way back, or what I thought was moonwalking, floating over the floor, I felt, and then I'd stop when the creepy, deep-voiced narrator came on and talked about the foulest stench filling the air, I'd stop real sudden and do my robot, mechanically popping and jolting because I was terrified of the song, the zombies and werewolf, and I had this idea that the more robotic and metallic I could get the more immune I'd be to their flesh-hungry teeth.

And then came The Helicopter, which was the pinnacle of my break-dancing routine. I'd yank off my shirt and let the music really start to flow inside, fill me to the point of animation, and then slowly, fluidly, I'd start to sway my shoulders, making sure to keep my arms noodle-like and rubbery at the elbows, and as I picked up speed my arms would begin to flap and the faster I'd sway the more my limbs would become a blur of flesh smacking and flapping at my shoulders as if motorized from my chest. When Michael Jackson got to the last few lines of *Thriller* I'd begin to slow it all down until I was swaying gently back and forth to the tempo, right in time, a miracle of flexibility and rhythm and *I* knew, even if it might not have been obvious to others, that I had just successfully helicoptered away from the death, the darkness, the teeth.

Aaron was a dancer, too. He was in a nearby ballet troupe and he knew all of the positions and he could do them all in a way that was every bit as good as the girls. He was the black sheep for a few years in our local production of the Nutcracker. The first performance he ran out in his costume and did all the wrong things, frustrating the shepherd, lingering when he was supposed to be offstage. I believed his deviation and inched to the edge of my seat thinking: *What is he doing?* But then the shepherd came out with her big cane and yanked him offstage as everyone erupted with laughter and applause. I realized it was all part of the play.

He had tights. He practiced at home in our room, pressing together his heels and rotating out his feet. First position. Second. Squatting. Jumping. He would dare me to say something, anything, and would threaten me even as he followed through, unprovoked, with body shots to my kidneys. He was good. At dancing, at hitting. He could have grown up to be anything he wanted.

We probably should have grown up to be housepainters, just like Dad. Painting is what paid our family's bills—most of the time. And Aaron and I helped out whenever we weren't in school at Love Inn. We helped cut in around doors and windows, unscrew outlet plates and light fixtures, putty in holes and endlessly sand. I was a miserable helper. Constantly making mistakes, creating more work.

Dad told me during one office-painting job to pry off the molding around the bottom of the walls. I didn't understand the vocabulary. I sat there with a five-in-one tool and yelled at him to explain exactly what he meant.

"The molding!" he shouted from the other room. "The stuff around the floor."

I took the five-in-one and jammed it into a seam on one of the black and white floor tiles and hammered it in, prying up the ceramic and grout. I hammered again and again, tiles breaking and piling up in shards.

I told him it was messy, that it didn't make any sense.

When he finally came in to check on me, I had pried away half of the room's floor tiles. I was kneeling with a hammer and a five-in-one and everywhere there was grout, dust, black and white ceramic in bits and pieces.

He was gentle that day. He walked over and quietly pointed to the baseboard tacked into the walls, the shoe-molding that he demonstrated would pop off easily, effortlessly, and told me to clean up the tile before I moved on.

Aaron was a different story. He was fast and efficient and before long Dad could give him entire rooms to himself, just let him go to prep and paint from start to finish. There was brief mention of adding "& Son" to the name of Dad's company, but Aaron wanted to do something more exciting, more himself, something as far removed from painting as he could get. And Dad, too.

Instead of shadowing Dad into the paint fumes we grew up and veered together toward the trees.

. . .

Aaron again dominated the speed climbing events on that hot Nashville afternoon. He was a fluid, freakish inchworm rocketing up a forty-foot line in under 18 seconds using the foot lock technique. He rang the bell at the top and he won.

He was also controversial, wearing a kayaking helmet instead of an OSHA-approved model. The judges talked briefly of disqualifying him for it, but my brother had a way of getting his way. He was now the number one competitor as we headed into the final Master's Challenge, a culmination of the day where the top four climbers from the preliminary events had twenty minutes to maneuver through a giant white oak, hitting stations spread throughout its canopy.

I was fourth. My aerial event went well. I placed the dummy safely on the ground, laid its Corn Flake head down as if I were putting a baby to sleep. Plus, I was fast. I had been on my brother's heels all day, not really wanting to win, not wanting to fall too far behind. Wanting him to be proud. Wanting to stay close in the same game.

And then I was sequestered behind a trailer with two other finalists while Aaron went to climb the white oak. I could hear the applause as he began. I could hear the individual shouts of friends and family, the erupting cheers as he found the first bell. It rang clear and loud through the cacophony.

...

Here's the thing about speed: when we lived in Freeville, we used to race down our country road on plastic three-wheelers whose jumbo black wheels rattled against the gravel. We learned how to spin out, do one-eighties, then three-sixties. We jumped them, launched them over boards leaning against teetering cement blocks.

Then we graduated to BMX bikes that our grandparents bought us from the box store in town. The biggest gifts we had ever received. Aaron's was black and yellow. Mine, red white and blue. We were allowed to pick our own and given plenty of time to make the perfect decision.

We went faster and faster. We pedaled break-neck to the creek whose current was lazy enough for us to wade into. Aaron told me about the fish beneath the water that had teeth like sharks and long snouts like alligators. He pretended that one had just bitten him on the leg, or that he was being dragged under the water.

In my mind I would beg: *Don't die, Aaron. Don't die.*

We'd pedal across the road to Kermit's farm, our neighbor, where a sea of corn waved in the wind, and beyond the corn, the woods. Two hundred acres of trees, at least. There was a junkyard in the woods where Kermit and his ancestors had dragged their old trucks and tractors to die, and then the trees grew up through the rust in the floorboards and out of the broken windows. We'd scramble to the top of the junk and pretend we were kings. We had swords of whittled hickory and we reigned over the woods.

Then Aaron would climb into the crowns of the trees and swing from limb to limb as if he had been born there and I would chase his shadow as it flittered over the fallen leaves. He'd hang from a high limb and say he was going to fall and I would feel like I was about to cry when, finally, he'd throw his legs back over and scamper to the trunk, laughing the whole way.

I'm talking here about acceleration. When we moved to Nashville condos we were suddenly surrounded by blacktop, so we got skateboards and learned how to manipulate them under our feet. I told Aaron to lie down on the hot asphalt one day, "Hold still, because I'm going to ollie over you on my skateboard."

"Okay," he said, "but don't fuck up or I'll kill you."

"There's no way I'll fuck up," I said, "because I can ollie over trashcans lying on their sides, over construction cones and boxes."

He lay down and I skated up the street, screeched the board around, and asked him if he was ready.

"Don't fuck up," he said and I knew he was ready so I started pushing hard and gaining speed, closer and closer to where he was lying on his back with his arms pinned tightly to his sides, his head craning to watch as I got closer, and then within a foot of his body I lifted up on the nose of the board as I smacked the tail against the blacktop, and I leapt with the board leveling itself under my feet just in time, over my brother's body, his head rotating as I soared so he could watch as I landed and then I disappeared down the street and he yelled, "Nice, man! You were really flying," and here's the thing about my brother and me: the truth is all we ever wanted, each in our own way, was enough velocity to fly.

...

Each station in the white oak was meant to simulate some kind of task a tree person would execute in a normal day of work. The Limb Toss required a climber to grab a stick from a suspended bucket and land it in a bull's eye painted on the grass below, which was not unlike the duty of avoiding a customer's azalea as you threw out a piece of deadwood. There was a station where a climber had to ring a bell using a hanging pole saw, and another where a bell had to be rung with a dulled handsaw.

And finally there was a station at the end of a long, bobbing limb which a climber had to traverse without putting too much weight on the branch, lest a plumb bob tied to the tip touch down on a buzzer below, snatching away crucial points. The Master's Challenge was over when the contestant zipped down and landed with two feet in the center of another spray-painted bull's eye before detaching ropes from carabineers.

Aaron, I could tell, had just touched down. Everyone was screaming because he must have nailed his landing, and he was on the ground after what felt like no time at all. Maybe ten minutes. It seemed like a record.

Two other competitors went in front of me. I waited. I heard the cheers and gasps. For one climber, the conspicuous absence of the plumb bob buzzer. For the other, the shrill electric buzz.

And suddenly it was my turn. I was escorted to the tree, allowed to gather my things, all my gear. I saw my parents, sitting awkwardly and silent on the same blanket laid out over the grass, my friends, the Eagle Scout. And then my brother, who had moved closer to the taped-off tree to get a good view.

"You got this," he said.

A judge had come over to check my ropes and harness, all my attachment points.

The tree was huge. Eighty feet at its top, at least fifty from side to side. I prepared my throwline in a loose coil on the ground to make sure it wouldn't tangle as I heaved it up and out. I spit on my hands and rubbed them together to make sure there was traction at my fingertips. The starting horn screamed and I immediately threw my line in a wide arc and missed the tree altogether. Then missed again. Everything in me clenched. On the third throw I hit a high fork, good leverage to reach the whole tree. I tied on my climbing line, tied my *Prusik* knot for fall arrest, and began the long ascent to the top.

I reached it quickly. I did this a dozen times a day, this ascension, this rising into the trees. I frequently forgot to look at the view. I forgot sometimes even what I was doing, settling into lofty branches simply by muscle memory, breathless, only to remember: *Oh yeah, I'm on the clock, climbing trees.*

That day I felt disoriented. I wasn't sure if it was the exertion from the climb or all the adrenaline. A few hundred spectators watching every move. I fumbled with knots and gear and remembered to search for the stations. I couldn't see them. I felt lightheaded, lost in the foliage, a jungle of green. I searched the distant crowd for my brother. There was a blur of color, a muddle of shouting and cheers. I yelled out his name.

"Aaron! Which way?"

I descended to the next tier of limbs and saw the first station. I could hear my brother screaming, confirming the limb. "That's the one!" he said. I scampered out and found a bell and a pole saw and I smashed the bell. The crowd screamed. My brother screamed. I worked my way back to the trunk and descended, frantically scanning for the next station. Aaron was yelling at me to stop, look left, and again I found a station, this time a suspended bucket full of colorful sticks, and far below, a spray-painted bull's eye. I threw one and missed. The stick went cartwheeling away. I threw another and it stuck, dead center. I felt good, then. More clear-headed. I zipped down to the next station, quickly rang the bell with my toothless handsaw and began working my way carefully onto the bottom limb, doing my best to keep as much weight as I could on my rope, protecting the buzzer from the dangling plumb bob. I was only twenty feet from the ground. I could see individual faces, hear all the cheers. Mom and Dad were there. From below Mom yelled, "Be careful, Josh," and I said, "I'm trying, Mom."

I stretched toward the station, fingered my handsaw from its scabbard and tapped the bell with the tip of the blade. No buzzer. I sheathed the saw and began working my way slowly back toward the trunk, yanking out my slack right-handed in order to keep my line under good tension. Finally, with one giant push from the tree I slid my knot down the rope and descended to the ground, landing with one foot in the target, one out.

And then there was cheering. Then there was my mom and dad running up to hug me. And then there was my brother, too.

The judges quickly tallied the points and made their announcements. Aaron took the championship. The best climber in the state. And then me: content, exhausted, unafraid of heights and a solid third.

...

We were always hungry for flight, each in our own way.

Aaron found the trees, a consuming world of wood in which the smells never washed from the threads of his clothes, the scars piled on top of scars until his exposed flesh—forearm, hand, below the ear and above the collar—was crisscrossed with red and white carnage, overwhelmingly scar tissue.

It's just that Aaron couldn't fly fast enough. If you're drawn to them, the sheer edges of life quickly lose their terror. You need bigger and more dangerous precipices.

Which is why Aaron realized that jumping out of airplanes might be the only thing to get his adrenals pumping again. He sought out a drop zone filled with kids who liked to live as hard as him. The day's dives in that small, Georgia airport were only the start of lavish drunken parties where everyone came together and unloaded all the tension and excitement of the day, mixed up all that waning adrenaline with drugs and liquor and waited to see what would come of it. The drop zone kids became something of a family to him. After a while I never saw him on weekends because he was gone, he was flying. He would come back to work on Monday and try to explain to the crew all about the thrill and speed and freedom.

I started having dreams of my brother ascending into the clouds alongside me, caught up for the first time in the same heavenly tractor beam I felt when I was five, only to plummet back to earth, head down, quickly hitting terminal velocity. In my dreams I would reach for him as he plunged, struggle and thrash against the upward pull in order to grab him as the gap between us grew.

One weekend my brother drove to the drop zone and felt particularly immune to death. Or perhaps particularly buoyant. Flight ready. Aaron filled his car with fellow divers and drove his car so fast and so full of his friends that when he got to the end of the runway, close to the place where the planes finally heave themselves into the sky, he caught his tires in the grass and began to slide. He compensated, overcompensated, and his car began to flip with everyone inside screaming and laughing because every day they lived as if it were their last. My brother was maniacal behind the wheel. The flipping was a beautiful thing. Three times over they went, all of them panting and shouting and so in love with life that the best way they knew how to celebrate it was to tempt death, say "Fuck you death!" as they tumbled violently through the air.

Aaron landed upright and rattled. He looked around at his friends and their eyes were giant and milky and glassy. He stumbled from the car and left it in the field at the end of the runway, bashed in and grass-stained, and he walked back to the hangar where he filled his head and heart with beer and everyone made love and passed out.

The next day the police came. They came for two reasons: one was to investigate the car crash at the end of the runway, and the other was to do their official duties in the aftermath of a skydiver who fell to his death as the sun rose. It was my brother's friend, the best of them all. Not just at jumping, but at everything. His friend who was the kindest and most caring, who treated the kids at the drop zone like brothers and sisters. The friend with thousands of jumps, a champion in the clouds, who that morning made a rookie mistake and lost his life the second he hit trees and terra firma.

My brother woke up, realized the loss, and surrendered to the police. He cried and laughed at the same time and felt deep inside that life was nothing but scar tissue.

Because he was the only one who knew such things, it was always my brother's drop zone duty to ascend the trees and reclaim all the canopy cutaways. Sometimes, when divers veered too far from their intended landings, there were bodies still attached, wiggling in their harnesses.

After his friend died my brother kept up his duties. Climbed high into the trees where the parachutes were snarled, carefully cutting them away. He would hang there and think of his friend sometimes, the thin cords of all those lost chutes fluttering in the breeze like corn silk, a rainbow of nylon brushing softly against his skin.

Five

I searched for and found the June 1971 issue of *Time* in which my father's picture appears. The cover story was "The Jesus Revolution," a long rollicking article that, according to the online archives, attempts to make sense of the waves and waves of young people recalibrating their lives to ancient Hebrew and Greek texts, moving into communities, shouting evangelical jargon from the rooftops and believing in a literal Christ who got himself literally nailed to a cross only to literally fly into the sky with the power to save the world.

The cover of the magazine depicts a multicolored, psychedelic Messiah floating in a comic book sky. It looks like a concert poster from the Fillmore West or Avalon Ballroom. Ironically, Dad's old blues band, AB Skhy, graced many such posters. But that was before Dad got a new gig, a holy gig, and somewhere inside that magazine he is smiling into a reporter's camera along with the Love Inn community of Freeville, New York.

"I was in that picture," he once said, as if I might not believe him. "With my afro bushy hair, maybe leather pants and maybe an army jacket."

He couldn't quite remember. He didn't have a copy of the magazine, which I thought was weird. Seemed like the kind of thing one would want to archive: the time I made it into *Time*. Kind of a big deal.

So it quickly became my archeological dig, my hunt for ancient familial artifacts. And although I thought it might take some time to find, as soon as I typed in the search box, up popped the issue on eBay, that giant hippy Jesus face hovering amidst clouds and rainbows. The Jesus Revolution. Three dollars from *gray7521* in Windsor, Ontario, and still six days before the end of bidding.

I waited. I didn't want to start pushing up the bids too soon. I imagined a small army of Jesus geeks sitting bleary-eyed at their computers, frantically punching the refresh button to get their winning bids in at the last second. How many other Love Inn kids were trying to dig into their parents' past, looking for that old issue of *Time* as a kind of Rosetta Stone, a key to unlock all the familial secrets, past, present and future?

Turns out there were only three others. And I kicked their ambiguously user-named asses. No mercy. The bidding hit $3.45, then $5.00, and then up to $9.01. But my willingness to pay up to $15 sealed the deal, and with a pounding and anxious heart I got the big eBay thumbs up, the green checkmark, *joshda1976* is the hands-down winner.

. . .

Dad left me a voice message not long after he sent me his *lettertoson.doc* letter. Well, not exactly a message, more like a rhythmic breakthrough rendered verbally into my phone. It was his way of reaching out. Since buying a used drum kit early in the nineties he had been innovating and manipulating his old beats ever since. He got excited about his breakthroughs. I was the one person in the family who could appreciate his percussive enthusiasm.

The voice message consisted of him *boom*ing (his rendition of a kickdrum), *chick*ing (the snare), *beeyoom*ing (tom tom) and *sheeyoom*ing (open high hat)—left on my voice mail, he said, so he wouldn't forget the pattern.

"*Boom-chick*...Josh, this is Daddy. Give me a call sometime. [a few seconds of silence] *Boom-boom, beeyoom... Boom-boom-chick, sheeyoom... Boom-boom, beeyoom... Boom-boom-chick, sheeyoom* [A few more seconds of silence, sound of fumbling with phone, high-pitched laughter, *click*]."

The total for the magazine, with shipping from Ontario, Canada, was $15.01. I forgave myself the penny. I was searching, after all, sifting through the pieces of my parents' marriage, anxious to see Dad back then in his *maybe* army jacket and *maybe* leather pants.

I had shoeboxes full of pictures, memorabilia (my dad's leather bell bottoms, a cracked Zildjian cymbal), an imagination full of stories told and retold a thousand times.

But for some reason the magazine had become important, an integral part of putting this fragmented puzzle together—my dad in his community, surrounded by believers, a small, long-haired army of people with: "A clarion call to broadcast and demonstrate the gospel of Jesus's love and power to change lives, to all the ends of the earth," Dad once told me. "It was on a banner in the barn quoting Psalms 19:4: Their voice goes out into all the Earth—their words to the ends of the world."

My dad, along with the rest, was shouting, singing, pleading with the world to take a look around and see the invisible hand of God becoming manifest exclusively in, well, them.

"We would all have agreed that we had been sovereignly brought together in time and history," he said. "To testify of our own experience with Jesus, proclaim the Word in lyrics, model the new life we were learning, and demonstrate the freedom in the Spirit to celebrate, have fun, and make great music to bless and entertain the audience, ourselves, and the Lord Himself!"

He believed. He was burning with it, that truth.

I just wanted to see the magazine and imagine what the bell-bottomed, afro-haired Terry would say to the man who had simply become Dad. I wondered what Old Terry would think of his present incarnation. I imagined the immense tether of time—day by day by day—between the two, and somehow wanted to introduce the distinctly different men to their season-stuck selves.

. . .

Dad slides into the plastic, bright orange Waffle House booth across from me and takes off his hat—a Sherman Williams baseball cap freckled with a thousand dots of color. His eyes are bloodshot and puffy. He smells like sweat and paint thinner. In the South so many things begin or end in Waffle House. Even dreams.

"What was it like, Dad, to be on stage back in the day? What did it *feel* like?"

"Crack, smash, zing, boom, blam, thud, blast, ping, ting, swoosh, swish, scrape, frap, smack, voom, zing again, double thud and SPLASH!" he says. "Now don't that *feel* good?"

He buries his face behind a Waffle House menu, behind glossy photographs of hash browns and meat and glowing glasses of orange juice.

"Dad, sometimes I think you're getting crazier," I say. "Maybe because of the paint fumes. You've painted a thousand little rooms with powerful paint and little ventilation. That can't be good, right? I had a friend lose her father when he painted in an enclosed room. Are you okay?"

He looks up, smiling, and shakes a cloud of dust and paint chips from his thinning gray hair onto the table between us.

"Repeat!" he says. "Fast, slow, medium, loud, soft, medium—paint cans could even suffice!"

"Dad, I think you might be fucking nuts. Sometimes I imagine you chewing on the leaded walls, tonguing the corners of the lead walls despite all the warnings on TV. You know that stuff will kill you dead, right? Or at least make you crazy, you glaze-eyed crazy motherfucker. How was it drumming on those stages, Dad? Tell me. Tell me. Tell me."

He grabs a fork in his right hand and a spoon in his left. He begins tapping on the metal napkin holder with the fork and his steaming cup of coffee with the spoon. The ride and the snare, the sizzle and the snap.

"Sound check," he says with a present tense look in his eye, as if he were right there back then. "We unload our own equipment from the truck, carry or roll it to the stage and begin to run wires, set amps, keyboards, and drums. We carry our own P.A. system, a Stramp 24-channel mixer made in Germany, and an ample set of speakers to handle a room of maybe two thousand."

"Amazing," I say, balling my hand into a fist and pounding the tabletop for the kick drum. I provide the base for his beat. The *boom* to his *bip*. The plates bounce with every thud and the servers begin to stare.

"Dad, sometimes I think you don't really hear anyone speaking to you because you always sound as if your words have been set on a loop," I say. "Sometimes I feel like I'm shouting into the canals of your ears but they're still ringing from your Stramp amp and now all you hear is rhythm and ringing and you've been breathing paint thinner again and I'm yelling at you but the cymbals have crashed into your ears where they shield you from all sound."

My dad stares for a second at his chopped steak, at the last little cube of meat drowning in a brown-gray sauce, then pokes at it with his fork like a cat batting at a fear-stunned mouse.

"Our bodies are created with rhythm and pulse," he says authoritatively. "Drumming is a glorious extension and amplification. Just feels good."

"Okay, okay, tell me more about the drums, Dad. Whatever you want to say I need to hear. Just tell me."

He sucks the cube of meat off the end of his fork and looks up, focused inward, as if he is trying to describe a dream from which he has just awakened.

"Mics were positioned inside the bass drum, over the cymbals, even on each individual tom-tom, hi hat, and snare drum," he says. "The sound engineer would fire up the system and ask for the snare drum—*plunk, plunk, crack crack*—he would get the sound and volume. Then the toms, the hi hat, and the Big Boy, the bass drum. It was fun. Because sound waves vary in height and weight, the bass or low register sound waves are big—move a lot of air. When I'd hit the bass drum, it filled the room, and you could feel it hit your body. Fun! It's kind of like the high notes (guitar, piano, etcetera) were the mist that hits you from the water hitting the rocks. The low notes were like being hit by the wave itself."

His eyes roll back into his skull and then close. His head sways serpentine, back and forth. He is lost in the waves.

"Say the prayer with me, Dad. Just once. Take my hands and we'll say it together: I invite you, Jesus, to be my personal lord and savior, and to come into my heart and forgive my sins and fill me with your holy spirit. Amen."

My dad's eyes snap open, then mine, too, and everything disappears.

...

It came! The magazine arrived. I sliced open the manila envelope, saw immediately that I paid $15.01 for an issue that originally sold for fifty cents, and fingered the pages feeling nervous and clumsy, as if I were touching old, brittle parchment. I reached the article, the one where my dad lived, but I decided to skip it for a while, fascinated by the context, by all the advertisements and articles. 1971. What a year. The Benson and Hedges cigarette company declared: "The longer the cigarette, the cooler the smoke." Two people hiked up a velvety green hillside, laughing, smoking, unwinded and in love. The Volvo Company said: "True economy isn't more miles to the gallon. It's more years to the car." And there was so much alcohol. Bourbon and rum and something called Triple Crown, which was designed with "the light drinker in mind." The bestselling work of fiction was *The Passion of the Mind* by Irving Stone. Sylvia Plath's *Bell Jar* was fifth. *The Exorcist* came in at seven.

It was clear in those pages that there was an intensified interest in spiritual things. In the metaphysical and enigmas of the soul. Everywhere portals were opening into other dimensions—through drugs, meditation, prayer. Poodle skirts were dead, road killed on a four-lane historical highway to altered consciousness. And the worldview that went along with those skirts had transformed into a searcher's free-for-all, a national sojourn for truth or pleasure or some kind of transcendence. Any kind of transcendence.

Dad once said of those days that there was a spiritual hunger among his peers. "A quest, pursuit, and books sold," he said. "All kinds of books, all kinds of gurus, all kinds of gods."

Of course the Jesus Movement folks capitalized the G, made it singular, and projected all that one-road-to-heaven dogma onto Christ, who they believed was personally available for intimate relationship as well as external change-the-world fireworks. For many of my dad's generation, Jesus Christ was the ultimate high.

The writer of the cover story, Richard Ostling, seems sympathetic toward the Movement. Even enthralled by it. He writes that the Jesus revolution was, "a startling development for a generation that has been constantly accused of tripping out or copping out with sex, drugs and violence. Now, embracing the most persistent symbol of purity, selflessness and brotherly love in the history of Western man, they are afire with Pentecostal passion for sharing their new vision with others."

I imagine my dad's generation overrun with slogans and posters and snake oil slingers on every street corner. Even so, Ostling still finds "an uncommon morning freshness to this movement, a buoyant atmosphere of hope and love along with the usual rebel zeal."

Morning freshness. The photographs back him up. Full-page, full-color shots of smiling, praying, weeping teenagers. A young paralytic flanked by hundreds of worshippers being carried into the Pacific for a mass baptism at Corona del Mar. A young man looking very much like the blue-eyed Aryan Jesus of Sunday school felt board fame "speaks in tongues," writes Ostling, "his mouth slightly agape, eyes closed, as serene as a stoner milking a high." A young girl in cut-off shorts and a shirt embroidered with *Jesus is my Lord* points her index finger at the sky in what Ostling calls a Jesus sign—a black power clenched-fist knock-off signifying a single way to heaven. Minus the erect forefinger, it is precisely the gesture I used to tell Aaron to stop the dump truck.

The article asks lots of questions. Digging. Is this all a fad? Is this just a religious Woodstock? Have these kids simply made Jesus into the image that most readily fits their generation?

Ostling thinks not. He cites the ways in which the movement had spread so completely beyond racial, social or class lines that it couldn't be an isolated fad. It was too viral, he writes. Too contagious. "This is a generation that has burned out many of its lights and lives before it is old enough to vote," he writes. "[The Jesus Movement] shows considerable staying power. It has been powerful enough to divert many young people from serious drug addiction. Its appeal is ecumenical, attracting Roman Catholics and Jews, Protestants of every persuasion and many with no religion at all."

One quoted lay leader says, "We are on the threshold of the greatest spiritual revival the U.S. has ever experienced."

And there was Dad in the middle of it all. In a tiny black and white picture on the top right-hand corner of page forty-seven. It wasn't a great shot. Although I was pretty sure it was Dad—sitting in front of the group smiling, his hands wrapped around his knees—I used the process of elimination to make sure, finding him by choosing who he was not. It was the lighting. His giant afro blurred into a dark shadow, making only the bottom half of his face visible. I could see his smile. And his mustache. And nothing more. The barn was behind him in full light, still early in its renovation, and the Love Inn community was spread around on a rocky hill with their arms draped around each other, laughing as if the photographer had just cracked a joke or told them all to say *cheese* or *whiskeeeey* or *Jeeeesus*.

...

I called Dad to tell him I found his *Time* magazine. He had no idea I was even looking for it so I had been kind of anticipating the surprise, relishing the chance to spring it on him.

He and Mom couldn't reconcile, couldn't get past his betrayal, so he moved out of the Sam Donald farmhouse into a tiny duplex in town and it had been a while since we had talked face-to-face. The last conversation hadn't gone well, so it felt as if we had been laying low, recovering from some of the more hurtful parts of the exchange. I might have called him an embarrassment, or something close to it. He might have asked why, if I was so full of venom, he should bother to talk to me.

He had called to leave me his rhythmic breakthrough and I thought the magazine spread out in front of me might serve as something of a relational bridge. I planned to tell him all about it but I got his voicemail: "Hello this is Terry. Please leave me a message and I'll get back to you as soon as possible. Thank you and have a blessed day."

"This is your son," I said. "I wanted to let you know that I found that *Time* magazine of yours on eBay and it came today. I'm looking at you right now, or at least the old black and white version of you. Let's talk. I never see you. Give me a call."

I hung up and wondered how long it would be before he called, and how I might answer when he did. Should I be serious and sober or should I joke around a little? Should I ignore the months of silence or should I put them right out in the open, poke at them like a kid with a stick standing over road kill? Should I tell him I had been practicing his new beat every day?

I waited for the return call. I waited five minutes, glancing periodically at the phone, sipping a beer and leafing through a New King James Bible my dad gifted me long ago. I waited ten, fifteen minutes. I got up and got another beer, checked the phone, and looked in the Bible's index for beer. Nothing. Half an hour later and I had meandered back into the Old Testament, which always put me on thin theological ice. I always felt a little vulnerable amidst the prophets, the creation story, and King David, the singing, dancing, murdering adulterer. I was never quite sure when I would finally read some obscure passage that would once and for all cut through the tiny ventricle of faith that still sometimes pulsated in my heart.

Instead I found Noah, whose story I seemed to read with fresh eyes: A crazy old man hears God's voice. He obediently builds a boat. He survives the humiliation of his people, the gossiping and sneers. He survives the flood, the day that "all the springs of the great deep burst forth, and the floodgates of heaven were opened." He steps out of that giant, rickety ark and, being a man of the soil, plants a vineyard.

Wine. Red? Muscadine? He drinks and he drinks and I felt glad he did, six hundred year-old obedient man, almost alone on a planet of bloated corpses, washed away bodies half-buried in mud and sand.

He drinks. He drinks until the campfire blurs at the edges, then begins to spin. He drinks until the memories of his friends left behind lose their sharp edges and no longer cut. He drinks and drinks until he can't stand the heat, all the warmth from the wine and the fire so he takes off his clothes and leaves them in a pile at his feet. He stands up with the fire reflecting off the sweat on his wrinkled body—six hundred-year-old flesh—and he twirls. Yes, he spins a little, worshipping and screaming toward the sky that he and his family are alive, and God killed all the rest, and the joy blends instantly with ache so he puts the goat skin again to his lips and slurps at the wine before stumbling to his tent, falling naked on the ground, firelight crackling against his ancient skin.

The sons. The three. First Ham, spared only to be cursed, opens the flap of the tent and sees his father snoring, still covered in sweat, still naked. And what does Ham feel? Does he laugh? Does he sneer? Is he fascinated to see his father's flesh in the moonlight and fire or is he embarrassed, the great patriarch laying before him drunk, snoring, seemingly half-dead?

Ham backs out of the tent and calls his brothers to him, but when they arrive, Shem and Japheth grab their brother by his neck and throw him to the dirt at their feet.

"You evil man," they say. "Why did you not cover your father's nakedness? Why do you revel in his drunkenness?"

Shem and Japheth take their father's garment, the one laying in a pile at their feet and, holding it between them, back into the dark tent. They sense their father's body behind them, can hear his heavy breathing, and with their eyes closed they lay the thick linen over his old bones and walk away.

Cracks of sunlight sting Noah's eyes. The morning has come too soon. His head throbs, his mouth is dry. He stumbles out of his tent and hears whispering, gossip, giggles. His granddaughter comes to him timidly, her eyes low, and tells him what Ham has done the night before.

Noah howls with anger. His blurry eyes suddenly focused on his surroundings, on Ham who is cowering in the distance.

"You are cursed!" he screams, flailing his arms as if casting a spell. "Your sons will be the lowest of slaves, your offspring will be enslaved to the offspring of your brothers for what you have done."

Six hundred years, one boat, no friends, and now three sons turned two. Whittled and whittled away.

. . .

When I showed Mom the picture of Dad in *Time* she laughed and said, "That's not your dad, honey. That's Joe. He was the best man at our wedding before he decided he was gay and left his family. Your father's not even in that picture."

She started naming off all the other people standing around and said again, as if I didn't hear the first time, "Dad's not even in this picture."

More names: Peggy, Pierre, Donna, and then for the third time she said, "Dad wasn't there."

At home I put the magazine on the shelf and picked up this picture of Dad I *knew* was Dad from a Sunday morning on Sam

Donald's farm, right after we finished a huge fight over coffee beans, as in where they come from and whether or not the ones we had just ground to make our morning coffee had come to us in a just and sustainable way. He was standing in front of the kitchen window. He told me to lighten up, that it was *just* a cup of coffee, and I got so angry I called him an idiot to his face.

He was getting ready for church. He had his black slacks on and a white shirt, tucked in without a tie, and he was barefoot, waiting until the very last minute to lace up his shoes.

I called him an idiot for not knowing that coffee was a hotly traded commodity, right up there with oil and weapons. "There is no such thing as just a cup of coffee," I said. And then I told him we were all American addicts screwing over the *campesinos* for our morning fix. I had just learned what *campesinos* meant a few days earlier in a documentary. I was testing out the word, the new awareness.

That's when he turned and went to the window, where the morning light wrapped around his body and ignited all the dust particles, where the light poured in and animated the steam curling up from his coffee.

He rocked back and forth on the balls of his bare feet, holding his mug with two hands as if he were chilled, as if he were trying to divine heat from the ceramic to fight off the cold. He was praying, of course, because that's how he did it, rocking back and forth, praying in tongues and singing, which means worship. He suddenly looked so beautiful and fragile and sad. I felt bad for calling him an idiot. I decided to take a picture of him, just to show him I still had a sense of humor. That I was sorry.

I snapped the picture and the flash ate up the backdrop of dust and steam, leaving just my dad. Just me and my dad.

. . .

One night I put on the album Dad recorded while he was clinging to a woman who wasn't Mom. He called it: *Mudpan Melvin and the Mission Blues Band.* He called himself "Mudpan Melvin." On it he has a deep, raspy singing voice that aches its way through the lyrics. A low, gravelly vibrato. I turned up the volume. He played polyrhythms on the ride cymbal and sang like mad. I felt my dad singing to me that night, through the computer, getting into my ears and singing so pretty and sweet like a serenade.

"We fear that silence is the voice of God," he sang, a tribute to Emmy Lou Harris. "It is the heart that kills us in the end."

I was standing in front of the computer, listening to my dad, listening to the drums and the deep voice and the frenetic tapping on the cymbal. And the truth is I still whistled the tunes to songs my dad wrote after his conversion to Christianity, the tunes he wrote to capture some of the excitement and joy and zeal of feeling like a kingdom had just set itself up right in his belly, on earth as it is in heaven. I turned his tunes into whistles and sometimes I sang the words, when I was out of earshot, I sang and I sang loud—from the treetops, feeding the chipper, on the staircase at the library, the one with doors at bottom and top, a chamber, really, that took my voice and hurled it against the concrete walls which deepened the tone and increased the volume and made it so my voice left my lungs only to come back amplified, vibrating through my bones. Sometimes I stopped there to hear my voice, singing my dad's words, catapulting through the corridor and coming back to fill my ears.

And he taught me the drums, used to let me sit on his lap as he drove the old Suburban around slapping paradiddles onto the steering wheel: *right-left-left, left-right-right.* He gave me some drums when he went to his duplex in town. I played his drums and I had this cymbal of his, a splash cymbal that cracked when he hit it too hard, and I had it attached to my kit upside down so I could see where he wrote in a Sharpie marker on its belly: *TA, 1991.* I turned up his song that night and I was fucking nailing that cymbal. A four-four signature. Simple. Rock and roll timing. I nailed the cymbal and beat his drums so badly I didn't know how they would survive and I leaned into the rhythm, the ride and the snare, the tom toms and kick drum, *Boom-boom, beeyoom! Boom-boom-chick, sheeyoom!*

My ears filled with my father's rhythm and Sam Donald's old walls rattled and my body erupted after another *thwap* on the snare.

Six

The modern arboriculture my brother and I practiced was rooted in the voracious hunger of a few parasites, *Cryphonectria parasitica* and *Ophiostoma ulmi*, the microscopic devourers of the once ubiquitous American chestnut and elm. The two species of parasite began to topple two of the most central and important tree species in American history, and thus birth the trade Aaron and I would one day inherit.

Chestnut trees were once foundational to every emerging industry, and were transformed by the board foot into fencing, rail ties, poles for the high-strung wires of telegraph and phone companies, electricity providers and streetcar operators. Chestnut bark was conveniently shot through with the essential tannin sought by leather makers, and the flesh of the chestnut tree was ideal for a thousand variations of furniture, from simple high chairs to elaborate paneling. By the dawn of the twentieth century, writes historian Eric Rutkow, "The lumber industry was cutting above half a billion feet of chestnut timber per year, the highest amount of any single hardwood species."

The American elm, too, had become central to the landscape, especially in towns and cities. My brother and I knew them mostly as challenging trees to climb. The elm canopy suggests "a fountain in its manner of growth," writes Charles Sprague Sargent, based on the way its trunk "...bursts into a sheaf of springing boughs, which again break into a shower of branches, with a spray of twigs...[that] produces at all seasons an architectural effect of permanent beauty by the arched interlacings of the great bending boughs."

For my brother and I, that simply meant it was rare to find an elm with a central tie-in point from which we could reach the tips of the long, bending branches in order to properly prune.

Because of its unique bouquet-like growth, writes Rutkow, elms were planted liberally along street sides, boardwalks and parks, where the canopies of two rows would eventually arch into each other creating a corridor, a mingling of "springing boughs" that Charles Dickens once likened to "…an old cathedral yard in England…a kind of compromise between town and country; as if each had met the other halfway, and shaken hands upon it."

The blights arrived in different hosts, most likely Japanese nursery stock for the chestnut, and for the elm, imported burls from France that contained both the fungus and the elm-bark beetle that helped spread it to the trees.

A small army of foresters and botanists stepped up to help discover, diagnose, and eventually destroy the diseases. These were the great-great grandfathers and grandmothers of our trade, the rambunctious climbers, surly loggers, and concerned, tree-loving citizens who veered away from the deep shadowy woods and humid greenhouses and blighted yards into the light of urban forestry.

By the time my brother and I took to the trees those blights had already feasted and taken their toll, decimated their respective tree species. Mostly, my brother and I were on alert for a new scourge, the emerald ash borer, another stowaway from the east toppling ash trees from the north, moving rapidly south toward Tennessee.

I used to sit out in Sam Donald's field and imagine the metallic-green insects fluttering from tree to tree, all the way from their American ground zero in southeast Michigan, making their way deeper south, singularly hungry for the ash trees surrounding the old house and Aaron's cabin, our fields their ultimate goal, the ridge upon which I used to linger.

The land around Sam Donald's farm, after all, had a kind of gravitational pull, a thick magnetism. Most of the major European powers—England, France, Spain—at one time vied for control of the area, after centuries of Mississippian-era Native Americans moved fluidly over the hills and through the forests. There was a time when Colonists fought viciously for the trees and fields, for their version of liberty, before finally settling upon the land to claim their reward—our ancient Nolensville neighbors.

From that ridge I also used to imagine what it was like for Sam Donald to first zig zag up the long gravel driveway. Only a few years before he purchased the acreage he had been confined in Bataan as it fell to the Japanese. Sam Donald the chaplain presided over the funeral ceremonies of 2700 of his fellow soldiers, he writes, many run through with bayonets, many more frozen to death or worked threadbare until they fell over dead. He would end each service with the Lord's Prayer and the 23rd Psalm: "The Lord is my Shepherd; I shall not want. He maketh me to lie down in green pastures: He leadeth me beside the still waters. He restoreth my soul."

I imagined this verse coming alive when he first saw the field, the oak tree, the smooth reflective surface of the pond.

He had been ordered to find a place of peace and tranquility to put his life back together again. The farm was his medicine, perhaps. His oasis. His happily ever after.

The Eagle Scout wound up the same driveway for the first time after walking fifteen miles down Nolensville Road one day, right through early afternoon heat, because he said the farm called to him. He followed the same bustling artery that a hundred years before was a muddy two-track running south out of Nashville.

My brother and I met the Eagle Scout at a downtown café where we mentioned the old oak tree we were using to practice for the next climbing competition. We came home from work a few days later and he was sitting with Mom in the kitchen, red-faced, waiting. Aaron immediately offered him a job and then the Eagle Scout never really left.

We had celebrations at Sam Donald's farm, parties that lasted for days. A New Year's Eve before our red oak uprooted we all gathered on the hillside under moon shadow, me and my brother and all our friends, and everyone brought their guns. We wanted something loud to close down an entire millennium and welcome a new one. We lay the guns out on a blanket and built a fire, feeding it until it screamed with heat and light. We took turns jumping over the fire so we could feel the heat on the bottoms of our feet and feel what it might be like to fall into flame. We were hungry for something ferocious to mark that night, something we could remember. We took the guns and pointed them at the pond where the turtles lived and we peppered the water with bullets, a bang and then a sound like suction and then silence.

We shouldn't have done it. Those were Mom's turtles down there, even though some were snappers. They belonged to her. But we pumped the pond full of bullets because we wanted so badly to make that night mean something.

When midnight came we decided to start running through the field, along the ridge, all together just bolting so we'd find ourselves in motion as we entered a brand new millennium, plunging ahead and alive.

The next morning we went down to the pond to see if we had accidentally hit the turtles but the surface of the water was as smooth and unbroken as a pane of glass.

. . .

When a tree is stressed and in decline it frequently dies from the tips down. Sometimes it will sprout suckers at its base to compensate for the loss of photosynthesis, which can make some trees looks as if they are skirted in green.

The adult emerald ash borer isn't a direct danger to the trees, but its progeny are deadly. The larvae burst to life beneath a tree's cambium and feed on its vascular system, leeching away nutrients and life pulse. The ash trees were dying rapidly from the top down, moving in on Tennessee.

My brother and I kept up our vigil.

When my brother and I cut down Nashville's trees we

picked them up with the crane and took them back to Sam Donald's farm to rest, dry, and eventually be milled into lumber, which we used to build things like benches or cabinets or small houses. It was a lucrative recycling. Paid to remove the board feet, gifted valuable lumber for the cost of running a mill saw over its length until round became square.

One day we brought the mammoth trunk flare from a cherry tree infected with bacterial canker home so we could carve it with our chainsaws into a giant chair. Aaron had a vision, and a buyer already lined up. I said I would do it even though I had never done anything like it before, but sometimes after enough beer I felt like I could do anything. I gassed up a Stihl 046 and pulled the cord and then circled the piece of cherry, doing my best to trace it with my eyes into a chair, to somehow spot the shape of a chair living within the mass of wood. I started sinking the saw into the hard flesh of the tree, trying to control the kickback, to keep the long bar of the saw from thrusting back against my face. Very quickly I had ruined the stump. It was chair-like, yes, but no sane customer would pay money for something so grotesque, all gouged from the chainsaw and misshapen. It looked like it was melting to one side.

I left the project alone for a few days, a few weeks, and returned to it to see if I could salvage anything. It seemed to limp and suffer more with every pass of the chainsaw, and each time I almost died a dozen times from kickback.

I left the farm that summer, bought a one way ticket to Europe with my tree money to see what I could see. Once I got home, I discovered the trunk completely disappeared beneath honeysuckle and weeds.

I had developed a habit of leaving the farm. It was appetite that took me out—although I wasn't quite able to name the hunger—and the same that brought me home.

This was coming home: the gravel driveway up to the farmhouse, a long obstacle course of ridges and potholes and startled animals darting in front of the headlights. Bits of rock pinging beneath the car.

The sun rising. Me stumbling through the front door and into the dining room, having been awake for two days or three days, and it's here I find Mom, freshly awake, clinging to me as if I were oxygen. She's so happy to see me, how 'bout some breakfast, some juice, a little coffee?

"No Mom, I've had enough coffee to fill a million years."

We sit out in the field and I put my arm around her. I see the old farmhouse still half-sunk in morning mist, the chimney almost completely gobbled up by English ivy. I see the stone wall, cracked from a thousand ice storms swelling in its joints, and beyond the wall I see steam rising from the backs of all the animals. I listen close and hear the low growl of my brother's dump truck warming up behind the house. I will go back to work tomorrow. Today is for rest, a Sabbath. I listen close and hear songs ringing in the throats of the birds.

The caffeine keeps me from sleep so I switch to beer, linger through the heat of the day, eventually go to sit in the field alone at night.

There are stars out and I can see them because Sam Donald's farm is so many miles away from the city. There are no street lamps here, just the dimmed light sneaking through the cobwebbed windows of my parents' house and Aaron's cabin. It is cloudless and by moonlight I can see the curvature of the ridge, and even make out the silhouettes of the animals grazing. I see Aaron turn out his lights and go to sleep in his cabin.

It is humid. I am sweating from the heat and my travels. I smell chainsaw gas and diesel and honeysuckle. I have a dark brown bottle of beer between my legs and beer on my lips.

I can see Mom walking around inside the house, feel the absence of my father. Everywhere the flicker of television.

"Sheep!" I yell, seeing if they will come to my voice, trying to get Mom's delivery just right. I see their eyes rise and catch the TV's glimmer, just for a second, before lowering again to the field.

...

The ash borer was still a few years from our border, although the blight would eventually descend on Tennessee's Smith County, half in the Highland Rim, half dipping into the Nashville Basin. From there the insects will eventually swarm the state, then the next and the next.

Back then the fields and forests around Sam Donald's farm were already full of nightly feasts, everything eating everything as if the acres themselves were created as a volatile recycler of all things. I used to go out to the field alone when I could hear the coyotes circling the ridge. Their manic yipping a kind of spiraling in, a shrinking revolution, closer and closer. We didn't own any guns ourselves so I went out bare-handed among the sheep and role-played the melee, tried to imagine how I would kill in hand-to-hand combat. I wondered how big their pack was and how many I could take out—five? Six? They were smaller than an average German shepherd, I figured. I did the math. My strategy was always to grab one by the hind legs and use it as a swinging bludgeon, bringing its body down on the others, skull against skull, until its limbs turned to rubber as it lost consciousness from the blows.

I was blood thirsty, those nights. Hungry for violence in a way that made me feel both electrified and unnerved. I wanted it. I was the farm's protectorate and I had buried the coyotes' half-meals all over the ridge. Tried to comfort Mom in the wake. I told my brother once that I had been imagining ripping a throat out, literally, and that after so much tree climbing I was pretty sure I had the hand strength to do it.

"Did you know coyotes are gods in some myths?" he asked.

"In other myths," I said, "coyotes are the creatures who made death eternal."

...

75

Mom loved life, believed it could reach into a heavenly forever, if only one believed. After her conversion she saw Jesus Christ as the once-and-for-all antidote to death and she wanted her kids to not only know that truth but propagate it as missionaries or chaplains, like Sam Donald. She didn't care if we ended up with college degrees but she relished the thought of us sharing the gospel to the far ends of earth, or shepherding soldiers through their violent storms. After leading me through the Sinner's Prayer when I was five, I was perhaps her greatest hope.

My sister, Amanda, was also a good candidate for a while, all through her teens, anchored as she was in youth group and short term trips to mime the gospel for strangers in European capitals. But her faith was crippled when she went to college and found parties and jam-band concerts more exciting than bible studies or prayer circles.

Aaron told me once that he had sought God with conviction a few times, reached out into the ether to see who would reach back. "Nothing," he said. "No one. I won't fucking fake it," and with that he put the whole thing to rest.

I tried so hard after my prayer with Mom. I would whisper to God when I fell asleep, again in the morning when I would wake. But then I began probing the silence, testing the invisible, trying to see if God would reach his heavenly hand into my tangible day and touch me, touch my world. I lay in bed one night staring at the box fan propped up in my window, and used all of what I considered my spiritual energy to get God to turn on the machine. For hours and hours I focused on the fan and believed as deeply as I knew how that God could, if he chose, do anything he wanted in this world, and that I, if only I had the faith, could move mountains.

"Literally move mountains," said my parents and Love Inn Sunday school teacher. That fan was nothing. A tiny little plastic knob. A simple click to power level three, then two, then one.

But the room was still that night, and every subsequent night I failed to turn on the fan with my own in-the-flesh hand.

My life after that prayer was a slow descent into unbelief. By the time we reached Nashville I had already begun drifting far, far away from that simple, child-like spark of faith, finding more peace and solace and excitement in psychedelics than the spirituality of my parents.

"Drugs are gateways for the devil," my parents reminded me one Wednesday before youth group, which I had been attending less and less. "Portals," they said.

But the portals were exactly why I loved them so much. Especially when a friend gave me a small piece of paper soaked in LSD. I thought briefly about my parents and their gateway speech but I was so curious, so hungry for a break or a respite or an escape that I sucked on the paper and within an hour I was stepping into a TV-like world, a surge of senses, everything throbbing, a gorgeous getaway from all things real into a kind of fantasyland.

I started eating acid as if it were aspirin and tried to live in the fantasyland forever. Jesus had nothing on those trips. At fifteen-years-old I tried to take it all seriously, too, read a little Timothy Leary, pretend I was some psychedelic pioneer working through important, meaningful, universal things in my own spinning mind. I felt, in fact, like I was finally reaching the real me, walking through the wardrobe and discovering the acid-drenched Narnia that had been there all along. Some nights I felt like I might have been the prince of the whole damn place.

Then one day I went to high school in that brief window when I actually attended classes and met a kid I'd never seen before. He had long, braided hair and he was wearing dark sunglasses. We were sucking down cigarettes in a little nook in the courtyard, scanning for teachers. He heard I was in the market for acid.

"Depends," I said.

"This stuff is intense," he said. "Straight from California."

I had never had California acid before. I nodded, asked him how much, bought two tabs.

I put the tiny pieces of paper on my tongue just before my last class so I would start to feel it by the time I was leaving for home. It didn't take long, though—there was a growing buzz halfway through English. I was staring at the scribbles of white chalk on the board—pronouns, conjunctions, an ellipsis—blinking furiously.

"Josh, you okay?" asked my teacher, who everyone called Coach.

"Sorry, Coach, just spacing out a little."

I was smiling uncontrollably.

"Try and focus, Josh. You need to get this right."

"Sure thing, Coach."

I rode home with friends. They wanted to play paintball and I told them they could play in our woods. "Just take me to my woods," I said.

I felt like I had lost my gravity, my earth anchor, like I was pressing harder and harder against the roof of the car, like if the roof wasn't there I'd rocket off into the atmosphere.

"I'll just hang out in the woods and watch," I said.

I was grinding my teeth, rubbing my thumbs hard against the fulcrum of my pointer fingers. My friends gathered their paintball gear and we all walked off into the trees.

"Can you hear me?" I screamed as they disappeared into the woods.

"Shut the fuck up," said a friend.

"I'm right here!"

"We can see you."

But I couldn't see them, skulking around in their camouflage, finding perfect brushy spots from which to snipe each other.

I went deeper into the woods. There were cabins back there riddled with loop holes where early settlers shot their rifles at the indigenous population. There were deer bones. Vultures in the trees.

I stared at everything and everything poured in through my

eyes. The world was inflating in me. I was blowing up like a balloon. That's always how it felt—it all rushed inside and I expanded with it but I never popped.

"I'm alone," I said to myself.

I heard the *thwap thwap* of paintballs flying by and exploding against nearby trees. There was the crunching of leaves as my friends repositioned, took aim.

I thought of my brother, my sisters, my mom and dad. Everyone close by, somewhere over the ridge. "I'm so high," I said.

Thwap thwap thwap!

It was true. The LSD was doing something different than before. I could feel it growing in me, the portal getting wider than it had ever been. I was way through the wardrobe, smack in the middle of the forest—*thwap thwap thwap*—I was so high that, for the first time, I was afraid I might never come down.

I looked into the sky. White clouds with blue in between. Look harder into the sky. Something changing. Something with my perception. Look harder into the sky and squint, try to get my vision to clear up again but the clouds suddenly lose their dimensionality and fall flat. Look at the trees and they are a glossy blur, the print of a postcard. Turn around 360 degrees, scanning everything, see a camouflaged friend darting from one surreal tree to another. Try to blink it all away but the disconnect is deeper than my eyes. It's behind all that, down in my brain or synapses or neurons. I never knew how any of it actually worked; it had always been so simple—take the tab, wait for the ride, go to sleep eventually and wake up back to normal.

"Oh my God," I said.

The trees began to decay from the tops down in real time, as if eaten by fire. Nothing but their bones remained.

Everything around me looked as if I were watching it through a television screen, watching myself through a grainy television screen. Then I closed my eyes and the screen clicked off and—this is real—I was trapped inside.

...

Aaron never really understood my geographic trips, although the psychedelic ones he frequently shared. I would pull out maps and try and show him where I planned to travel, how I planned to do it, and he would sometimes humor me and pretend he was listening for a while, but mostly he ignored me.

It wasn't missionary work but it was at times humanitarian, a reaching out, an attempt to serve others, a value I still clung to, even if I was pretty sure Jesus wasn't working through me with some kind of divine purpose. It was just me, I figured. Other times my travels were completely self-centered. I baked bread for refugees in Albania and dug a new sewer for orphans in the capital city of Kazakhstan, and I drank unwisely in Denmark and lost myself at music festivals in southern Hungary.

I would come home and Aaron would let me slip back to work without filling out an application and I would climb into the trees with a chainsaw until I had just enough to launch myself back out, endlessly up and out.

Sometimes I wished my brother would join me, that maybe he would feel the world move within him as it was for me. I had started writing on those trips, feeling like suddenly everything had a kind of importance. All of a sudden it was worth capturing. I wanted him to feel the same thing, but he was myopic about his work in the trees, and the fun he could purchase around town and at the drop zone with the proceeds.

I wrote to him from internet cafes. Wrote to Mom and Dad and my sisters. Told them where I was and what I was doing. Transferred horrific poetry from my journal to the screen and hit send. Described cobblestones and beggars and cathedrals and sleeping on the deck of a ferry surging over the Adriatic in the middle of the night, thinking endlessly of what was next, and also of returning home.

...

I had started calling it "My Walk to the Woods." Describing what happened there brain wise—I mean the actual physiology of it—was beyond me. I tried with my mom, my friends, my brother, kept talking and talking: "It was a hit of acid at school bought from a kid I had never seen before, a walk into the woods where friends were shooting each other with paint guns, a weird feeling in my stomach and a glance up at the sky and then, suddenly, everything just changed."

It's when I tried to explain the change part that I lost myself in abstraction and faulty metaphor: "Something clicked in my head. A switch went off. Life went from three-dimensional to two. I deep-fried some synapse that I was never supposed to touch."

People nodded and made sympathetic *uh-huhs*, but I knew I hadn't gotten to the heart of it. Or how desperate I felt. No one knew about the thoughts of suicide except Mom. I would sit at the edge of my bed and cry and she would put her hands on my head and pray. She told me I needed to pray, too, and believe that God would turn the lights back on and, just for a second, I thought she might actually get it—a darkness, yes. It was like a darkness. But she forgot how many times I had already sat on that bed's edge trying to talk to God, or how I pretty much stopped believing in him years ago when I chose sitcoms and acid over Wednesdays at youth group.

God, I discovered, doesn't flip switches, doesn't turn on box fans. The lights didn't come back on for me. I was scared, so scared I would go out into the field at night and ask a God I didn't really believe in to descend or move or do whatever it was he *did* do for people—to come and heal. I told God I was thinking of taking my life, and that if he were real, I hoped he would have mercy on me for such a serious sin if I met him at the gates.

It was fall and I was so young and the leaves of the forest looked as if they were smoldering. One night I left Sam Donald's farm and went to Waffle House where I could sit and smoke. I sat in a booth at the back corner because it's where I had been sitting forever, and hours went by as I watched people making love to each other with their eyes over coffee, people ending relationships, christening new ones. Someone was yelling Nietzsche quotes at his helpless-looking friend and everyone was starting to act crazy because it was Halloween and late, almost late enough for the bars to close down, which is when Waffle House transformed from a simple diner into a crazed circus.

I was sitting in my corner sipping coffee when a man in his mid-thirties walked in with dreadlocks down to his waist, these long black tendrils of matted hair. He glided in and sat down and I was so comfortable in that place that I almost felt like it was my living room, so I walked over and said, "Man, nice hair," and tried to make conspicuous my own dreadlocks, which were really just a few tangles sprouting from the top of my scalp, tied up with my mom's hair tie. He looked up from his menu, smiled and said, "Thank you." I went back to my booth and drank coffee and filled my lungs with smoke.

A few minutes later I saw Dreadlocks stand up, pivot on his feet, and look right at me like he was looking through me, or into me, and then he walked over to my booth with this weird smile on his face. I had been around that place a long time. Seen so many crazy things and crazy people. I was braced for anything.

But he just stood there at the end of my booth and looked at me with that same deep down stare and didn't say a word. He was towering over me.

"What's going on, man?" I said, but Dreadlocks was silent. Just stood there. And then he got this big smile on his face, like he had finally figured something out, and he sat down right across from me and said, "You know why I'm sitting here, don't you, Josh?"

It was no dream, no trip. The words slid from his throat and, somewhere in the smoke-filled air between us, grew into a locomotive that smashed into my chest. As real as anything

I had ever known. His words pressed me back into my plastic booth and pinned me there. A flood of tears. A gasping for air.

"Yeah, I know why you're here."

And it's true. It had only been a week before and I had been outside in the field trying to give my parents' God one last shot, the God I had asked to inhabit my heart when I was five. I spent all night outside along the ridge, waiting, and when the sun finally came up and I hadn't received any divine signal I slugged Nyquil and crawled into bed and knew I had the courage to die.

Now it was a week later and Dreadlocks was sitting across from me at Waffle House, telling me that God heard me and that, in fact, God knew all about my pain, the damage, the fear.

"God was listening, Josh," he said, leaning in. "God actually heard you. And he's heard you from the beginning."

He kept talking, laying out my whole life in front of me. He was telling me things that no person could possibly know, secret things about my hopes and fears, things I hadn't even told my brother. Dreadlocks was looking inside me with an x-ray vision and gently going down the list of everything he was seeing. And then a server came over to refill my coffee and froze with the pot, right at the end of the table, and he started weeping, too. There was an electricity in that corner, hovering over our booth, and it started zapping everyone around us. I had been in stadiums full of drugged people spinning beneath multi-million dollar light shows and never experienced anything so powerful.

"What should we do?" I finally asked.

"We should go outside in the parking lot," Dreadlocks said. "It's quieter out there."

I looked around and saw some of the servers in drag and everywhere women dressed like witches and fairies. The whole diner was staring at us. It was Halloween and the air was charged and it felt as if we were all tipping into some other dimension.

So I stood up and walked outside with Dreadlocks. The server did the same, set his still-full coffee pot on the table and followed. And we all huddled together, right underneath the giant yellow glow of the Waffle House sign and asked Jesus to come live in our hearts and never leave. A repetition of the same prayer, the same words, the same sentiment, separated by a dozen or so years. The dazed adolescent channeling the little boy on the edge of that bed.

"Do you feel different?" Dreadlocks asked when we had finished.

I didn't know what to say. I tried to get inside my head and inspect my synapses, look around the parking lot to see if everything still looked two-dimensional. There was the soft yellow light coming from the Waffle House sign. There was a buzz deep inside my body, maybe adrenaline, caffeine, maybe something more.

"I feel different," I said.

"That's the Holy Spirit," he said. "Everything will be different now."

I believed. We all exchanged telephone numbers, wiped away tears, then drifted off in different directions, still a few hours of Halloween left before sunrise.

The next day I told my brother that I met Jesus last night at Waffle House, that it was for real, and that everything was going to be different now. We stood there by the dump truck for a few silent seconds. He set his ropes down and took his pointer finger and jammed it against my chest like he was trying to break me open and see inside.

...

I burned through my tree money in Europe and Central Asia and Australia until I had just enough left to buy a one-way ticket home again. I would check my account in, say, Helsinki, see I was down to a few hundred dollars, and buy a ticket back to Nolensville and the farm and the trees. So many times leaving and coming home.

But Jesus was now infused in my travels. I was a messenger

for a gospel newly alive in my head and heart. I never considered myself a missionary, more of a Jesus-follower looking for opportunities to reflect him. That's how I thought of it then.

Mom and Dad had yet to split that Halloween and they rejoiced together. A resurrection! A new beginning! Dad told me one night that the most Christ-like thing I could do was to rejoice with those who are rejoicing and grieve with those who are grieving. We were watching the evening news where we saw a story on Chechen refugees fleeing the Russian military and then a story of more refugees in Kosova fleeing a Serbian genocide, flocking into Albania where they had set up camp in the capital's main square.

Grieve with those who are grieving, rejoice with those who are rejoicing. Be there, on the ground. Be there inside the news stories. Step through the screen, pour yourself out. Like Jesus. Be like Jesus.

I tried hard. I tip-toed over border crossings as a new believer—a re-ignited one—flashing my worn passport, knowing I wouldn't try and save anyone's soul but that maybe God could still use me somehow. He was real, after all. He had met me in a Waffle House on Halloween night, cut through all the cigarette smoke and chaos to pluck me out. Earmark me for his purposes. I figured God was most preoccupied with the poor and suffering so that's where I went. To be preoccupied, too.

But I was hungry only for what seemed real and raw. No Christian gloss, no churchy facades. I could only believe in a merciful messiah if I went out and allowed the world he had come to save pour into me. All of it. The darkest parts and beautiful parts had to overlap, intertwine, knot together.

I would come home from my trips and tell my brother about the kids on the streets whose parents had drugged them in order to generate more sympathy and generosity from passersby, how they lay in the sidewalks on cardboard with their eyes wide open, staring at the sun, sunburned pupils, sunburned skin, grimy palms open for change.

"Fucked up world," Aaron would say.

Or the death camps I visited, and the pictures of all the victims ground up in dictator machines. Jesus had to be real in those halls and in those chambers, I decided. I had to be able to worship him standing in front of a mountain of discarded leather shoes piled high behind the glass.

"Her name was Irena," I told Aaron once, referring to the picture of a girl with a lazy eye taken in black and white, hanging among thousands at Auschwitz. Irena Dutkiewicz. I had written it down in my journal, along with a terrible poem I scrawled in her honor. And her number: 63383, and the dates she was at the camp, 16-9-1943 – 24-3-1944, before she was gone.

I felt like I had to put people like Irena and the children I had met on the streets in conversation with Jesus. I kept trying to imagine what he would say to them, or what they would say to him. *Where were you?* I imagined them asking the savior. *Where were you when I needed you most?* And then I would imagine the text from my parent's poster in the bathroom back home, the one where God said that when you are struggling most in your sandy journey, when it looks like there are only one set of footprints on the beach and you are walking alone in those tumultuous moments, that's exactly when I am carrying you.

But that was already starting to feel kind of bull shitty. Especially sitting next to a comatose child baked by the sun and used as a flesh-tool for money gathering. More and more, my imagined conversations between victim and creator had God turning directly to me and asking: "Where the fuck were *you?*"

. . .

I was looking everywhere for God. At Sam Donald's farm I sometimes imagined him living in the trees along the ridge, tangled in the leaves whispering divine secrets, if only I had the ears to hear. I knew that the priests of ancient Greek myth listened for Zeus's voice—his will—in the rustle of oak leaves.

From there they would interpret it into sprawling screeds for the people. I knew that, according to scripture, the trees of the fields were supposed to clap their hands in worship of the living God, that even the rocks were poised to cry out in adoration as the fronds of palms padded the way for the King of Kings, who was on his way to be nailed down to a smooth, draw-knifed tree carcass. He would bleed into the grain but he would rise again and then, for a tiny window before he rocketed off to the heavens, we could press our hands into the holes in his hands and we could know for sure he was real. Then that window snapped shut.

I used to think of Sam Donald and his oasis, surrounded by the forests with their decaying cabins, think of the tree limbs stacked in pyres over which Old Testament sacrificial bulls burned into ash, an incense for God's hungry nostrils, for God who wanted to destroy us and our sin but who couldn't smell the sickly scent of our transgressions because of all that burning wood and steak. "Atonement," it's called. I imagined the trees of the fields crushed endlessly into paper where my shitty poems were beginning to take shape. I was forever scratching into tree flesh trying to make sense of it all. I thought of the Ash trees growing straight from the grave in Sam Donald's old fields—root, cambium, leaf, breath, life. The ash borer moving closer, bearing down. Tree roots cradling the bones of dead sheep and rabbits below. The trees of the fields full of gods and spirits, Dryads for the red oak, Meliai for the endangered ash. I imagined the Meliai furious over the emerald ash borer, the infant insects feasting under the bark, larvae gorging and gorging until the host finally surrenders. The Meliai die when their host trees die, according to the myth, and Aaron and I were sweeping through Nashville trying to get ahead of the plague, looking everywhere for signs of ash decline, decapitating the trees, chipping them away, trying to stem the plague's flow which was a new hunger surging down the east coast—tiny mandibles munching. I was home and already wounded from the world I

had set out to explore and my brother and I tore through Nashville destroying the Meliai who screamed at us and swarmed us
and tried to pull at our hair and beards from their tree tombs. I
hadn't found God in the children on the sidewalks, couldn't be
him for them, couldn't see him through the thick cast iron of
the ovens of Auschwitz so I sought him in the trees and sought
him in my brother, for my brother, through my brother there
was a god moving through the trees destroying and feasting and
never resting in the tops of all the ash trees bending down low
in decline.

Seven

I was sweeping through a line of hackberries trying to detangle and deadwood, prune and organize, when my Nextel flip-phone buzzed in my cargo pocket. I burrowed my hand between my harness straps in order to grab it, flip it open, answer the call. A Washington D.C. prefix. I had been waiting for it all week.

"You've got the Russia assignment," said the managing editor of a magazine I had queried. "You can connect with the group in New York, and from there you'll fly to Moscow."

I slapped the phone shut and howled from the top of my hackberry.

I had practically begged the managing editor to let me have the story: a trip to Russia to visit orphanages and highlight Christian efforts among the kids. An honest-to-goodness byline in a glossy magazine. The editor had asked for a writing sample, as I hadn't published anything but my name on credit card receipts, so I wrote an essay hoping to prove I was at least literate, peppering my sentences with words like "Orwellian" and "zeitgeist," hoping it might do the trick.

Strangely enough it did. I screamed at my brother in a nearby tree that I got the gig and then zipped to the ground, as if I might leave immediately.

It took a while longer. After a month I flew from Nashville to New York and met a small group of evangelicals who had adopted the cause of Russian orphans condemned to a state-run existence of predictable meals and innocuous surroundings. The evangelicals were looking for media attention for their efforts. That was me: Media Attention. They were creating the story and it was my job to capture it.

After leaving the trees behind I remember trying to calculate exactly how much metal it took to whisk me from Nashville to Moscow, and from Moscow to that grumbling Russian bus. The planes themselves were hardly comprehensible, those immense, two-story fuselages, all the rivets running like goose bumps down the sleek metal wings. There were the airports with their turnstiles and kiosks and columns, and then that bus, so blackened by diesel exhaust and *gryas*—Russian for "mud"—that the bright red metal was almost unrecognizable.

We had reached the region of Kostroma—an orphanage—where my bus emptied quickly of its passengers, a dozen American evangelicals scouting out Russian ministry opportunities, and me, the full-time tree climber, pseudo-journalist, and confused-Christian hired to cover their exploits.

So as the kids swarmed us that day in Kostroma I tried to do what I imagined my job to be. I thought: Great photo ops! The kids jumped into the eager arms of the Americans and writhed around, trying to absorb every last ounce of love and warmth before their teachers came to pull them away. I furiously snapped photos with the fancy film camera my brother had loaned me before leaving, the one he used to capture before-and-after pictures of our jobs. After half a roll I wandered off into the leafless trees and snow. In only a few days I was already anxious to escape the Americans.

It was dark. The sun had been absent since we arrived but I didn't miss it. If it were to peek through the clouds it would have seemed unnatural and out of place, like a white-faced clown at a wake. It had been a tough week, more disturbing than hopeful, despite the efforts of our little troupe of believers.

As I walked further into the dark, a hundred yards from the bus, I saw a small girl hiding behind thorn trees and cedar. She was standing perfectly still, motionless, and I soon saw why she was hiding. There was a boy only a few yards from her, standing behind another tree, waiting. I stopped to watch them, unsure if they were playing a game or if it was something more sinister. I wasn't sure if I should step in and rescue the girl. They had yet to see me and they remained completely still, even though light snow was falling all around them and covering their feet.

I moved closer. The girl was wearing a bow in her hair, and

her arm was locked around a colorless stack of schoolbooks. The boy was standing erect, proud, his chest thrust out and full. He looked awkward among the thorns. And something was wrong with him. When I looked closer at his face, I saw that it was missing, erased, as if someone had taken a chisel, placed it on the bridge of his nose and with a wallop knocked all the features onto the ground below.

The girl. She was white, the color of snow and the impenetrable sky. She was looking at the boy, but part of her face was missing, too. Her eyes were still there, staring blankly, but her nose had crumbled away and there were deep pockmarks cutting into the skin. Her free arm, the one without any books, was missing from the elbow down.

Then I saw. She was stone. A statue. And he, too, was fading granite, falling away in bits and collecting in rubble at his own chiseled decaying feet. They had been locked in that position for years and the orphanage children had been harsh to them, beating their stone features away with bricks and rocks and wooden sticks.

I greeted the stone children, touched their damaged faces, traced my finger along the girl's neck where a jagged crack revealed she was once decapitated and sloppily repaired. I turned and walked back to my companions, still tangled in a mass of children and, because of the dim light, flipped open the flash on my brother's fancy camera.

. . .

The orphanage, unlike all the mechanisms that had brought me to it, was a remarkably non-metallic place. A world of wood constructed mostly by hand-tools and sweat—the windowsills and floors and the crossbeams of the ceiling. The hundred or so children who lived there slept in cheap wooden bunks. Heavy pine shutters locked securely over the windows, doing their best to fend off the winter wind.

The only color in that place was dull and cracked, barely clinging to its wooden surface. If someone decided to paint a windowsill red or green or blue, it had been many years since the chore was finished and no one had gone about touching up the color since. My dad might have been helpful. The long Russian winters have little mercy on color.

We all gathered in a long wooden cafeteria, a too-warm place filled with the all-female orphanage staff dressed in white aprons, some with their heads wrapped in handkerchiefs. Only the director was male, conspicuous in a cheap suit. I could see that his teeth were a mixture of gold and off-white because he looked me in the eye and smiled wide. He shook my hand with a firm grip and patted me on the shoulder, pulled me close and whispered in my ear as if I were the only one in the room he could trust. "Comrade," he called me.

This was the place where day after day the kids came for soup and sandwiches. But only the nurses and teachers were there tonight, scrubbed and stoic, sitting silently in a row on one side of the room. The Americans occupied the opposite side capped in baseball hats, colors and name brands. The director sat in the middle of the horseshoe with bottles of vodka, sweating profusely, and I had scooted my chair away from either side, toward the door, to breathe fresher air.

The room was hot. Vodka was tickling our veins and the multilingual volume was growing. The director was especially animated. Every few sentences he erupted from his chair and spoke with sweeping gestures, flashes of his hand, his gold-ringed fingers. He had unbuttoned the collar of his shirt and loosened his tie. With a theatrical wave he dismissed a nurse to his office with instructions to bring more vodka to the table. His face was a deep shade of red. He was an inebriated ringmaster.

Tonight the vodka was flowing for nurses and teachers as well. The evangelicals had come again, after all. It was their money that had paid for the kids' new backpacks and coloring books and, in defiance of winter, would soon jumpstart a new round of painting. The evangelicals were like royalty or rock stars, sweeping through the orphanage a few times a year for a few days at a time, handing out candy and doing puppet shows, practicing the Russian niceties they had learned from their phrasebooks: *spasiba, zdravstvuite, puzhalsta.*

Tonight was an event, and the director wanted to make sure it would be memorable. He shot to his feet and said there was to be a song. His intention, I think, was to provide a truly Russian experience, a late-night peek into the musicology of the motherland. His hounds-tooth arms snapped out and the nurses and teachers sat up straight and silent with military-like precision. The director had transformed instantly from the ringmaster to the conductor, his stiff arms suddenly fluid at the elbows. Under his guidance, robust Russian patriotism flooded the room in four-part harmony as each of his staff sang with force and conviction. But his guests weren't listening. Instead they were already plotting out which quintessentially American tune would outdo the singing of their Russian hosts.

The evangelicals pounced on the silence, shouting out a slaphappy version of "Take Me Out To The Ball Game." They were on fire, burning from the vodka in their stomachs and the smoldering drive to win a contest of their own invention. They were throwing their heads back as they sang and pounding the wooden table with their fists. As they finished, the Americans unleashed a flurry of high-fives and *whoops,* flailing their bodies on their long wooden benches.

The nurses sat in rapt attention, quietly waiting their turn. And when it came they settled on a solemn number in a minor key. They were serious about their music. They sang the unintelligible Russian lyrics with a kind of sadness, an earnestness. The exertion was making them sweat. They finished their song and began fanning their faces, leaning forward in anticipation. They had given it their all, put all their cards on the table and now anxiously awaited the unveiling of the American hand.

The evangelical trump card was "Swing Low Sweet Chariot," a sloppy version sung wildly off key. Their collective volume built in increments until the last stanza was shouted more than sung.

And who can stand up to such enthusiasm? Who can compete with the childlike fervor, the sheer energy that these Americans—these evangelicals—bring to their crusades? The resurrected Christ was in these people, after all, in them to save the souls of these orphans and in them to sing their Russian hosts into the cold, winter-swept ground.

A flash of movement sparked in my periphery. I turned to see the eyes of three children peeking in from the room's only entrance. They were only a few yards from my chair and I could see the mops of their hair and their tiny fingers curled around the doorframe. They were soaking up the room, every sound and color, the smell of the soup and alcohol.

This was our audience. They had witnessed this trouncing of their staff by the Americans and they would whisper about it tonight in their bunks, telling their wide-eyed neighbors how red the director's face looked and how the nurses and teachers fanned the sweat from their faces after singing their sad, patriotic songs. Every sight would be remembered and recounted to disbelieving friends underneath old, woolen blankets.

These were the children the evangelicals had come to save. At the time there were over 800,000 of them in Russia. Their lives stunted the second they entered a state-run orphanage, such as the one we had just infiltrated, even though over ninety percent had living parents. They were there because their parents lacked the money to feed and clothe them, or were too hooked on drugs and alcohol to be real moms and dads. They were there because doctors had noticed a stutter, a harelip, a slowness and diagnosed them *oligophrenic*, literally "small-brained," encouraging their parents to give them over to the state. And they were there because Russia has a long history of institutionalizing children, rooted in a not-too-distant past when gangs of parentless kids—the *besprizornye*—were swooped up by the Bolsheviks and sequestered in orphanages, places where they could be kept free from the dangers of the bourgeoisie; a generation of children raised according to the paternalistic standards of the Kremlin.

One way or another, they were all considered orphans. And how does one describe 800,000 children? You can choose to see them as a great mass of souls, their young lives devoured by a monochromatic childhood of meals, bedtimes, beatings. Or you can try to see each one, each face, count their fingers and toes and know their names. Alexi. Sonya. Katja. Some were smeared with snot and filth, their faces locked in expressions of perpetual disconnect. Others were sharp-eyed, pensive, processing their surroundings with all the insight of social scientists. Still others were deviants, sexual predators or bullies, preying like wolves on the weakness of their orphaned friends, even their own brothers and sisters.

The gospel has something for these children, said the evangelicals. *The hairs of their heads are numbered in the eyes of God and each is loved by him unconditionally. It is through us believers that God will save these kids and bring hope to their lives,* they said. *If we choose not to obey, these kids will die in darkness.*

I was struggling daily to trust this same God. My involvement with his Kingdom since Waffle House had left me feeling confused and, at times, concussed. It's true that on the first page of my notes, as I was waiting for the plane to carry me from New York to Moscow, I scrawled a type of prayer to the God I assumed I had begun following since my second Sinner's Prayer. I wrote that I was scared of being exposed as a fake journalist and bad Christian. I asked God to give me peace, strength, and protection for the journey.

But I had a bad habit those days of talking to God mostly when I needed his guidance, or when I was overwhelmed with fear and anxiety. Any expectation that he had both the power and will to save Russian orphans from their statistically bleak fates had started to exceed the granule of faith I kept in my pocket, the one I sometimes ground between my thumb and forefinger when I got scared. I was quick to accuse God of falling asleep at the wheel and running his planet into a cosmic telephone pole. I couldn't stop playing the human prosecutor grilling the divine defendant, pointing to the detailed evidence of his failures, calling up a growing list of expert witnesses: the orphans of Kosova. The orphans of Kostroma.

The director was still sweating. A deep red rimmed the lobes of his ears and brushed his cheeks, his nostrils. He was whispering again with his staff, discussing song choices and keys. He felt like he was losing control, I think, animated to the point of anger, dismissing a nurse's recommendation with a rapid shake of his head and a sharp wave of his hand.

Earlier tonight, this same director insisted that 100 percent of children who "graduate" from his orphanage land real jobs in the real world. His kids are trained as bricklayers, seamstresses or house cleaners, he said. They leave his compound with the skills appropriate for entering an explosive economy such as Russia's.

His mathematics were common among the Kremlin's orphanage directors, who provided perfect reports and described ideal conditions, even as the walls of the kids' rooms crumbled. There was hardly a second thought given to the veracity of such numbers. The directors offered them flippantly, as if they were common knowledge. These were bureaucrats who had spent most of their careers as Soviets, after all. These were men and women who had mostly known a political and social culture in which the truth was subservient to propping up the Kremlin's onion-domed façade at all costs.

The truth, I eventually learned, was that many of Russia's orphans were ejected from their orphanages, at fifteen, sixteen, at seventeen years old. They were stigmatized by the world outside their wooden and concrete homes, dismissed as faulty, unwanted, even animal-like. Graduation was an occasion for fear and mourning, not celebration. They were thrust into the world with few marketable skills, scarce legal options for entering society, and the black mark of *cirata*, "orphan," stamped conspicuously onto their papers. The people most excited to see them graduate were pimps and drug dealers, a new kind of family, a new community with big plans and hollow promises.

God and I never had much of a honeymoon. These Russian children joined the refugees I had seen in Albania—some still bleeding from their war escapes—and the children buried beneath rubble in the earthquakes of Pakistan, Turkey, Chile. These were the witnesses I called before God the defendant in order to ask why the walls caved in or the bullet struck or their clothes were torn away by wolves.

Of course I was already used to God's inversion of the questions, his redirecting them at me, but in Russia I imagined him pointing hopefully to the colorful evangelicals bouncing all over the country, buying backpacks and saying "hello" and "goodbye" with clumsy accents and no knowledge of Cyrillic script. His people. True believers. His army of earth-anchored hands and feet.

Outside the building, across the snow-swept yard and curled into their bunk beds, were hundreds of children loved by God and those who heeded his commission. Tonight, only three had ventured out, walked over the snow and found the courage to peek in from behind the doorframe. They were bold, entrepreneurial, adventurous. They caught me watching them so I smiled, letting them know I wouldn't be the one to rat them out to the staff.

I wanted to celebrate these three kids. I wanted to let that night belong to them and them alone. They were the champions of the day's story—it was all about them. The small orphanage, the snow, the statues and wood and warmth all revolved around those tiny adventurers. The sad, patriotic singing of the staff was their theme music, sung just for them, sung in minor keys with robust Russian sincerity.

I glanced back and they were gone, shooting across the orphanage yard and into their bunks. The snow would quickly fill in the depressions left by their shoes, erasing their intrusion forever.

When it really fell, the Russian snow was virtually opaque, a solid wall of white. Everything in Russia seemed impenetrable. I had circled the walls of the Kremlin on my first day in the country, felt weirdly panicked as the great gates snapped open without warning, releasing lines of black Mercedes and BMWs that slithered into the streets of Moscow.

And then there were the bureaucracies these kids would have to someday navigate, the stranglehold of Soviets-turned-oligarchs over the economy, the environmental devastation of Cold War catastrophes and contemporary disregard. Even the physical cold seemed dense and impassable.

I first learned of the Russian cold from a young Siberian named Tanya, who explained it in detail to Ryszard Kapuscinski, a Polish journalist wandering the Soviet Imperium with the curiosity of a child and the pen of a poet laureate. In the account of his travels, he writes of Tanya's town sinking slowly into the tundra and of the little girl jumping over puddles, hopping over the evidence:

"What's your name?"

"Tanya."

"And how old are you?"

"In two months I'll be ten."

"What are you doing?"

"Now? At this moment? I'm playing."

"What are you playing?"

"I'm jumping over a puddle."

"And you're not afraid that you'll get hit by a car?"

Tanya giggles.

"No car is going to be able to drive through here."

The naïve journalist knows nothing of the fact that her world thaws into mud every spring, sinking in seasonal increments further and further into the Siberian ground.

Kapuscinski asks the girl if she's at least afraid of catching a cold, which ignites her discourse. She explains the nature of *real* cold, describing how on particularly frigid mornings the fog gets so thick that a person walking through it will leave an impression, a long corridor through the crystallized mist. She can look out of her door in the morning and see if she has to go to school merely by searching for the corridors of her fellow students, the tall impression of her teacher in the fog. If it is unbroken, she goes back to bed.

"Sometimes one sees a corridor that is very crooked and then abruptly stops," she continues. "It means—Tanya lowers her voice—that some drunk was walking, tripped, and fell. In a great cold, drunks frequently freeze to death. Then such a corridor looks like a dead end street."

This is how I would begin my story, I decided, my article. Tanya and the fog, and then the analogy to the social freeze these orphans would face. I made furious notes. I was on assignment, a bona-fide journalist, dammit, and the rounds of vodka had warmed my writing hand. The scribbles and diagrams poured over the page like webs. The names Alexi, Sonya, and Katja darkened as I retraced their edges with my pen, mumbling the word *oligophrenic* to get the pronunciation right, imagining a graduation day where no one comes to say "well done."

...

We all woke the next morning with pounding headaches. It was early, still a little dark, and roosters were exploring the timbre of their voices just outside our dorm window. The night had ended in a crushing defeat for the Russians. The director and his staff simply crumbled. Every attempt at outdoing the sheer energy of the evangelicals was overwhelmed by the Americans' volume and the pure singability of western pop music. Frank Sinatra made an appearance. The theme song to Rocky was shouted— no words, just the melody—and ancient Christian hymns became weapons in the throats of my American companions.

We dragged ourselves out of bed. Our Russian driver had

already warmed the bus, scraped away the ice and snow and positioned it close to our dorm where we could all shuffle easily from our bunks to our seats, close our eyes, and allow the giant diesel motor to escort us to the next orphanage.

The children from that place had pressed together in one giant mass of bodies to see us off. They shouted and cheered and clapped, jumped up to the windows and slapped at the glass. They smiled and waved and some of them cried. Some of the Americans cried, too. One woman on our bus said, "They're just like little birds," and her eyes were filled with tears.

We had a few more stops before returning to Moscow where we would board our plane for home. I had tapes full of interviews, scraps of paper filled with my attempt at shorthand, rolls of film bulging in my brother's camera bag.

I also had no idea what I was doing. I was no writer. I had never successfully completed a high school English class. Before leaving for Moscow I rented *All the President's Men* to see what journalists did, to sit at the feet of Robert Redford and Dustin Hoffman and study their gestures and posture. I had leafed through a *Complete Idiot's Guide to Grammar and Style*, forgetting everything I read within minutes. This was my training.

But as we passed more woods, more highway, a million more miles of snow, I wondered if it were possible to fake one's way into authenticity, to play the role until it was real. Watch the movies, act it out, sprinkle in some tenure and there you have it: legitimacy. I wondered, too, if faith might work along similar lines. It didn't matter that day. As our bus cut through the fresh snow of the next orphanage's parking lot, I simply grabbed my brother's tree camera, started taking pictures as we were greeted at the front of the giant, concrete building by what looked like a military procession, a well-scrubbed column of orphans, all in their teens with exaggeratedly perfect posture, and a line of teachers and nurses dressed in starched white uniforms. Towering over them all was a woman, a female director in a role normally reserved for men, dressed in a fashionable suit with short-cropped hair.

My American companions and I stepped from the bus and into the blinding white snow. The children received their cue and began to sing while each staff member stepped forward individually to shake our hands and welcome us to their building, which, upon entering, we found had been scrubbed clean and deodorized. The noxious smell of bleach stung our noses and throats as the director lead us to our dorm rooms and told us to rest before dinner and a dance party that would be held in our honor. And everywhere along the halls the little faces of children peeked out, giggled, and whispered to us. The kids sang phrases in English, blushed, and then disappeared into their classrooms and dorms.

My brother's camera captured them. The film caught glimpses of their lives, their faces, and at the same time protected me from both. I could stare through his upgraded lens and fiddle with the aperture, focus, shutter speed—*Click*. The roll advanced automatically and I moved on, too, searing their faces onto the film and sparing myself from having to look too closely or for too long at their eyes. So many beautiful, distinct sets of eyes.

That camera also protected me from the evangelicals. It separated me from their agenda and their tactics, drawing a vocational line between us that was reinforced every time I pulled the apparatus from its bag and loaded a new roll of film. I was not there to save anybody's soul or pull anyone out of the pit of hell. My confidence in God's followers had been shaken as much as my infant faith in him. If God was at the wheel, these believers of his were certainly in the back seat, shouting out all the wrong instructions and throwing candy wrappers and plastic bottles out the windows. I had seen their ranks in white face paint miming the gospel to refugees in Albania, and I had seen them fusing nationalism with their faith by supporting war overseas while overlooking the "least of these" back home. I had decided I was pretty sure I wasn't one of them. Sort of. I was only there to take the pictures and tell the story. They could pose with the kids, hold them up to my brother's lens, and I would simply press the button. Everyone smile. Wipe the snot away. Steady. *Click.*

...

Russia was the bulls-eye on a million evangelical maps long before the Soviet Empire crumbled in 1989. For decades, the most radical a Christian could get was Bible-smuggling into a communist country. It was one thing to claim Jesus as living in your heart, but something entirely different to smuggle his written word past the stone-faced, rifle-wielding guards at Soviet borders. The Christians who took the risk for the sake of the gospel were like evangelical Special Forces, a small elite that sought to look the devil in the face, fake left, and give him a swift kick in his fiery red balls.

When the Empire finally fell, its walls crumbling beneath sledgehammers, bulldozers and a million clawing fingernails, an evangelical free-for-all swept into the vast country. God had finally opened the door, it seemed, and invited every American evangelist with a pulpit and enough money for a plane ticket to come spread his or her version of the gospel among the communists. It was part carnival, part crusade. And although almost a million orphaned children languished in prison-like conditions while the great hall in Moscow was rented out for glitzy, multi-media evangelism services, Christian ministry in Russia *did* eventually filter out to the kids, to the prisons and prostitutes. Trickle down evangelicalism.

And there we were.

We were unloading our bags in a giant room filled with old military cots. Green fabric stretched taut over metal tubes. The cots all sagged deeply in the middle from the hundreds of bodies and the hundreds of nights—restless, violent nights—when soldiers tossed and turned the stiffness out of the fabric, making it supple, soft, like thick green tissue.

Our pre-dinner tour was about to begin. As I stepped out of the room with my brother's camera bag I felt a small, soft hand close around my own. A young girl dressed in an overwhelmingly frilly blue pantsuit was staring up at me, her smile a delicate crescent on her pale face. Her white sleeves billowed around her bone-thin arms. She looked as if someone had tried to dress her up like a little doll, the kind they sell to tourists on the streets of Moscow.

"My name is Sasha," she said in bold, choppy English. "I am ten years."

I curled my fingers around hers until our hands locked into a traditional handshake. I pumped her arm in an exaggerated way, up and down, side to side.

"*Minya zavoot* Josh," I replied, smiling. "*Kak de la?*"

Sasha refused to respond to my strained Russian with anything but her clipped, courageous English.

"I go with you," she said, again wrapping her tiny fingers around mine and tugging.

I realized the possible meanings of her words. She could simply have wanted to go with me on the tour, or she could have wanted me to take her home, be her father, buy her a closet-full of frilly pantsuits.

"Ok, you go with me," I said, assuming the former and allowing her to tug me down the hall after the Americans and the director, who cast a long shadow over us all.

Sasha never let go of my hand. Into every classroom and around every corner she was my guide, gesticulating with passion each time her words failed her. She showed me the saws in the woodshop and the sewing machines, the places where the youngest kids slept and her own dorm, scrubbed clean and filled with bunk beds. She followed me to dinner and pushed her way onto the seat next to mine. She watched me eat.

It was getting late. The night closed around us. And then Sasha was towing me into the stream of bodies headed toward the lobby for the dance party. We all funneled into the giant room, its forty-foot Soviet ceiling supported by massive marble columns. Someone switched off the lights and the music came. It was a kind of clanging Russian pop and it rattled from a large boom-box set up on a radiator. It was loud enough to make us feel surrounded by the beat, enclosed, even though the speakers were buzzing from the strain.

Suddenly, Sasha was dancing. She was twirling. She had let go of my hand and was bouncing around me like a float, up and down and side to side. So I started spinning too, bumping into the tiny bodies of orphans and stepping on the toes of the evangelicals. And it was so dark that I couldn't really see her anymore and I couldn't see the kids whose bodies were swirling around mine. I was struck by something like vertigo, losing track of where I was and with whom I was dancing. It felt again like being at the top of that competition tree, screaming for my brother, asking for directions. Which way? What's next? The room spun and I spun too. Dizzy, reeling, losing track of Sasha and her puffy white sleeves, lost without my little guide and her funny blue pantsuit.

I stopped, stood still, and my brother's camera bag swung into the small of my back. I pulled it around and dug through the contents until I found my headlamp. I flipped the switch and the sharp blue light permeated the lobby. In an instant I saw a hundred gyrating bodies illuminated by its LED glow. I held it at arm's length above my head and surveyed the room. I looked down and saw Sasha at my side, staring directly into the light. She had stopped dancing. She was as delicate and mesmerized as a moth. I saw the director, who had grabbed one of the evangelicals by the hips and ground her body into his. Their eyes were tightly closed. I saw all the kids in a frenzy, bouncing and diving and circling each other like fallen leaves re-animated by the wind.

The light was shaky in my hand, pulsating through the room. I realized that by swinging the device back and forth I

could create a disco effect, a quality of light that captured everyone's movement in tiny flashes, robotic gestures, stop animation.
The kids screamed with delight. The music pounded and the
speakers buzzed. I was in the center of the room turning in a
slow circle, swishing my headlamp side to side and up and down
while Sasha clung to my sweaty hand, circling with me and staring at the light—my little guide leading me around and around
through the black, dizzying Russian night.

When the lights finally came back on, flooding the room
with detail, the dancers were breathless, hot, teetering as if they
had been spinning and suddenly stopped only to find the world
still at it. The director was panting and her hands seemed reluctant to let go of the hips of her partner.

But the lights were back on and the mood had changed. Sasha, though, was still by my side. Her devotion was unbending.

When she walked me back to my room, she explained that
she would write to me and expected me to write to her. She also
made it clear that she expected me to return. It struck me that
she had moved beyond the naïve notion that someone would
actually stick around. She knew I was transient. She had undoubtedly known many of us. She had become adept at attach-
ing herself to our hands for a brief moment, perhaps in an attempt to get at our hearts, to ensure that we would return. Or at
least send a letter.

"Good night, Sasha," I said.

"Good night, Josh," she said.

"I'll write you a letter," I said.

She smiled, squeezed my fingers, and walked quietly down
the hall, her pantsuit swishing around her skinny ankles.

Sasha's name slipped into my notes. Such morbid notes. I
had statistics on STDs and violence, and the exact number of
UN articles on the rights of children that Russia's state-run orphanages violated: 20 out of 41. There were instances of children being tied to their beds, sequestered from their friends,
and of staff who encouraged older kids to enact violence on

their younger peers. I knew that sixty percent of the girls who left orphanages would become prostitutes. I knew that seventy percent of boys would become homeless or live in a jail cell. I knew that fifteen percent of those kids would simply end their lives within the first two years of graduating.

I wanted to keep Sasha away from my notes. Even the letters of her name seemed vulnerable in the midst of such numbers. The numbers seemed to close in on her name as soon as I wrote it on the page. She was hunted, stalked.

Such thoughts robbed me of sleep. I rested in fits and the morning came too quickly. The bus's motor had been idling for some time, heating up the pistons and making the vinyl seats warm to the touch. Again the kids had gathered around the hulking metal thing with a kind of end-of-the-world energy. They were laughing and cart wheeling and throwing hard-packed snowballs at each other and the evangelicals. Sasha caught me as I exited the building, wrapping her thin arms around my waist, pressing her face against my stomach. She spoke to me in Russian. Too quickly for me to make out the words. I could feel the vibration of her voice through my clothes, through my skin. I bent down, put my arm around her shoulder, pressed my face close to hers and for the first time turned my brother's camera on myself. On me and Sasha. *Click*. Now I was in the story too.

...

Our bus rolled slowly away, crunching into a fresh shelf of snow. I put my face against the window, resting my forehead against the cold glass. I watched the kids falling over themselves and running ahead to the gate where they joined hands and formed a human chain in front of the bus. They were smiling and laughing and kicking snow at the bus driver. Sasha was there. She was trying to keep us there, too. She gripped the hands of her friends with cold, white knuckles until the staff and teachers came and pulled them all away, scolding and smiling at the same time, waving apologetically and scurrying the kids off to the side. We waved goodbye. We were getting used to this. We were getting good at this. We were gone.

The second we reached slushy asphalt I pounced on our team leader, Tom, whose dark beard was growing beyond its neatly trimmed borders and whose eyes had a penetrating effect, making me wonder if he was looking through my wool sweater and seeing the imposter just beneath. I pushed my tape recorder close to his face to block his view.

Tom was a young American Christian who felt a divine mandate to help widows and orphans. He had written a book and spoken at a thousand churches and conferences, and he had made it his life's work to come and help these kids. This was his trip, his mission.

My recorder captured his voice, his passion and energy. He was hard-wired to excite. Five minutes with him was like a semester-long lesson in hope. He said his work with orphans was the "pure and undefiled religion" described in the New Testament book of James. He was out to change the course of the cumbersome evangelical ship, he said, to reset the rudder and head due east for the orphanages of Russia, the Ukraine, and Belarus. He had brought countless Christians to these places, allowed the children to swarm them and crawl into their laps and watched their hearts break wide open, he said. Their checkbooks had opened, too, and been filled with the wet scrawl of big numbers. He had helped to shake American congregations out of their myopic concerns over tithe and attendance and given them a real mission, something tangible, something they could sink their teeth into: pure and undefiled religion.

"It's easy to have an evangelism crusade," said Tom. "The hard thing is getting in the boat with people, getting our hands and our knees dirty with them." He smiled brightly, widely, sincerely.

I liked Tom. I couldn't help it. I trusted his authenticity and in many ways I was still trying to *be* him, looking for ways to make the gospel work in real time, in real life.

"When you look at the life of Jesus he spent his time touching the leper and having the children come to him," Tom continued. "It's that unbelievable touch ministry that made Jesus who he was. That's what he calls us to do."

Tom was good with the kids. He knew what delighted them. He had little tricks, like pulling a *kopeck* from behind an orphan's ear or making funny sounds with his mouth. He high-fived and yodeled and filled a room with joyful screams. But he was also serious. He said that at one orphanage he didn't trust the director. He said the director was squandering the orphans' Kremlin budget and the kids were suffering. He said there were ways of ousting such a director. Tom had connections and he understood Russian bureaucracy even if, after all those trips, he still hadn't learned the language.

I kept thinking of the different flavors of following Christ, how in Nashville, Christianity could be so clean, hip, and marketed as if it were the next big thing. On a single stretch of interstate, church billboards in my city were at times indistinguishable from those advertising the grand openings of shopping malls and steakhouses.

But then there was Tom who loved the kids. They were in his dreams. They crawled into his lap and worked their way into his heart and smashed it to bits, broke it wide open. He was raging against the numbers in my notes: sixty percent prostitute, seventy percent homeless, fifteen percent razor to the wrist. He was trying to save Sasha, to pluck her delicate name from the numbers and give her a fighting chance. He had developed postgraduate programs, job training initiatives, and safety nets. He got the kids out of orphanages and into real homes with caring families. He looked *through* the kids and saw his savior, Jesus, in their elaborate threadbare clothing. *What you have done for the least of these you have done for me.* He looked into their gleaming, colorful eyes and saw his benevolent carpenter king. He loved them. He loved Him. They were all on their way to heaven.

As for me, I wasn't sure I ever wanted a dragon-slaying messiah more desperately. I wanted the life version where villains always get their punishment, the good guys always conquer. Those orphanages and their tiny inhabitants made me long for that extant king, for that in-the-flesh savior who calls the little children to him because he has counted their silky hairs and loves each one. And he will keep them safe from the predators.

What both frustrated and encouraged me was that Tom might be all the world gets. And what downright terrified me was that I might be all the world gets, too.

...

The revolving doors of the Moscow Hotel opened into what looked like the brightly lit food court of a fancy shopping mall. You could buy a gin and tonic, a cashmere scarf or an expensive box of imported chocolates—all while waiting for your credit card to electronically cover the $200-a-night hotel room. But these were just diversions. Tom and the evangelicals were magnetized to their rooms and the promise of the first hot shower in days. They navigated the lobby like robots calibrated to comfort, their *go* knobs locked securely on "sleep." We would all be home tomorrow.

But I was coming alive, waking up. I could see Red Square from the lobby, and I could hear the sounds of a million people and their machines bottlenecking through Moscow's streets. I gave myself over to the frenzy.

I passed Lenin's tomb, forever guarded. I zigzagged over the Red Square bricks where soldiers once marched and missiles rolled in front of the cameras, terrifying my country and my childhood: *If the Russians attack, drop under your desk and hold your knees to your chest and don't scream...they might hear you.* I went underground, under the city and into the maze of tracks and corridors that connected dilapidated neighborhoods with Moscow's center. I knew that the Kremlin went underground, too, deeper and deeper into the earth with every new wave of paranoia and secrecy and purge. There were cavernous rooms as big as buildings down there, and tiny cells the size of coffins. Back above ground I walked quickly through the streets, pretending I knew where I was going. I didn't stop for directions or advice, just pulled my jacket close around my body and neck and walked rapidly into the wind, rapidly through the Moscow gray.

I was alone for the first time in days with no one to interview, no journalistic duties. My brother's camera now collected little bits of architecture and the Russian anomalies peeking through all the snow. Here was a statue of Marx staring sternly past a digital flat-screen two stories tall, erected across the street, filled with quick-edit gaudy advertisements and color. Here was an old woman, a babushka whose life fit neatly into a wobble-wheeled shopping cart, and speeding past her a 22-year old in a Maserati. Here was the goliath Church of Christ the Savior, a wonder of 19th century architecture built to celebrate the Russian defeat of Napoleon. The czars created it, Stalin turned it to rubble, Khrushchev reshaped its bowels into the world's largest swimming pool, and Yeltsin resurrected it to its former glory. It was the largest church I had ever seen. And here was a line of women standing awkwardly in a row, shivering, wearing mini-skirts and halter-tops despite the cold. Here was a man with a cheap digital camera waving them in front of his lens, wait for the flash, *Click*, move on. I imagined their faces published on a website where they would be sold west as loyal wives.

Anomalies. And yes, some of the mini-skirted women were undoubtedly orphans. The orphans were everywhere. They graduated in waves, 15,000 a year, and poured into the dark cracks of that city where they lived or died according to the hands into which they fell.

But, God help him, Tom was in that city too, trying to be the one who caught them. And there was all the staff he had cobbled together to help protect those kids. Tom was waiting for them because he loved them and they held his hand long enough to smash up his heart. He stopped prosecuting God and just listened to the kids and now he ousted directors and bought new backpacks and pulled *kopecks* from behind their splendid tiny abandoned ears. He was defying winter by putting new color on the old wooden windowsills and he was working hard to keep the wolves at bay.

I was done. Exhausted. I passed heavily back through the neon lobby and into the carpeted halls of my hotel where it was warm. I was filthy and needed to thaw. I had more information in my head and unease in my heart than I could process in a hundred years.

And as I walked past the lobby I began seeing the young women, the girls who would like to take me into their rooms in exchange for enough cash. I had never seen women like this. I had never seen seduction or sex so flaunted, so openly on display. They were like mannequins from the greasy windows of red light district novelty shops. But they were real. And they were everywhere. Each one looked as if she wanted to take my face in her diamond-ringed hand and kiss my lips—for a price. I could feel it. And I could hear their offers in heavily-accented English, promises of a good time, an hour of ecstasy.

I wanted to think there was some sadness there, just beneath the surface of their velvet voices, or longing for rescue, or dreams of a different life where they wouldn't have to service politicians and mafia and the American sex tourists who flew over an ocean to get at their bodies.

I could only guess. I couldn't get past the surface—the jeweled, china-doll surface.

And yet there was a woman leaning close to my door, her cheeks flecked with glitter and her eyes rimmed with dark mascara. I felt ashamed to look in her eyes but I did. And I looked closer.

And then I saw. She was Sasha, but her pantsuit had shrunk to reveal her legs, no longer bird-like, and the puffy sleeves had disappeared to show more of her milky white skin. Her hair was the same; blond and thin with shiny bangs cut straight over her brows.

But her smile was different. The crescent of her lips was now angled down on one side, crooked, collapsed. Her smile meant something different here than it did in her orphanage.

"Welcome to Russia," she said, warm and sensual and inviting.

Her words sailed from her throat and caught in mine. I looked quickly away. I fumbled to slide my card through the door's scanner and took only the imprint of her face into my quiet room, where I could see the Moskva River and all the lights caught in its wavy current. Lying in bed, the lids of my eyes sinking from exhaustion, I allowed her delicate features to shuffle into the snapshots of all the kids I had met over the last week, all the other women waiting in the hotel halls, the babushka and her wobble-wheeled shopping cart, Tanya and her crystallized mist. Such a loaded deck. So many singular, lovely faces.

Click. Lights out. Eyes closed. 800,000 children blended dreamily into one, into my courageous little guide who never let go of my hand. She was dancing, spinning, twirling down the hotel hall, her clothes shrinking against her skin as she went. She stopped outside my door and propped up one of her long, slender legs, leaned against the wall. Her other foot planted firmly on the carpet and her eyes stared blankly ahead. I saw her delicate, soft features slowly harden into stone and begin to crumble. I saw men snaking down the hallway, lining up to touch her hair, her face, her throat, even though their fingers would move on before ever knowing her story.

My name is Sasha, she whispered. *I go with you.*

Eight

Dad always called Nashville a boom town. When he first suggested we move there from tiny Freeville I imagined a cityscape suddenly exploding. Boom. Town. Nash. Ville. Skyscrapers consumed by flames.

He was talking about the economy, of course, and all the new construction, a city seeping out of its own borders into the surrounding cow fields, a thousand newly constructed bare walls ready for fresh paint, a faux genius.

And he was right. The city daily, hourly crept further and further into the countryside. We could feel it getting closer to Sam Donald road, even though we were thirty miles south and sandwiched far away between two interstates: I-24 and I-65. My brother's dump truck commute into Nashville used to be primarily pasture and woods. We'd hit the interstate and still have a slow lane pastoral ride into town.

But Nashville was like a giant dandelion sitting tall in the Cumberland Valley, and it seemed to propagate malls and retail and big box stores like blown spores. Neighborhoods took root and devoured trees and fields. Roads widened and straightened. Fresh asphalt. Clean lines of paint. Long crane arms and half-constructed condos became downtown's new skyline. The night sky out at the farm got brighter and brighter, too. The stars dimmed. For a while we could get to town faster than ever before, then fresh traffic started to gridlock all the acceleration.

Nashville was always a city brewing in expectation. Something was eternally and imminently on the horizon. The city was forever on the threshold of being the next Vegas or Chicago or Paris or Amsterdam or Hollywood. Industries were poised to explode and bring the city world-class status. Everyone was talking about everyone talking about Nashville. The people flipping hash browns at Waffle House were on the cusp of fame as singers and songwriters. Everyone poised. Everyone hopeful.

Everyone expecting and waiting and busting their asses in the meantime.

Nashville was booming. Nashville was on fire. Nashville was so sweltering hot.

I would stagger home from a day of work, a day of what always felt like a physical impossibility—cranking through the heat and humidity, defying gravity, not dying—and assess the bodily damage. Feeding brush into a chipper demanded a kind of bear hugging of abrasive material. Then shoving. Most days it looked like I had spent the work hours running razors not-so-delicately over my flesh.

I never took stock of injuries during work, as there was never any time to stop, and everyone pretended to be indestructible anyway. The pain of any individual wound was muted by violent labor in what felt like a wet oven shot through with machismo. We were everywhere punctured. Sliced. Burned by the sun. We all pretended not to notice.

But all the wounds found their voices with that first shower. Everything begged to be known and accounted for. *I am here!* screamed all the cuts and bruises.

I would tend to my injuries as the city inched closer and most nights I felt desperate to go out and meet it. I scrubbed myself clean and headed into town, sometimes just to Waffle House but other times driving around, a hundred miles in a night, waiting for something to happen, waiting at each stoplight for signs and divine signals.

The city felt like a souled thing. I was in love with it because of its familiarity and heat and lushness and I hated it because it was so rich and opulent and I had seen such poverty. I drove around the wealthy parts and imagined all the grand churches falling in on themselves, or street children flooding the pews.

I drove around on those late-nineties nights and Nashville was full of honeysuckle, which for me emitted the smell of expectancy. I figured something would soon happen when I smelled it. Nashville had honeysuckle on its breath. Nashville was bright-eyed and sultry. Nashville was so hopeful. So sweet. So hip but not really. Naïve and full of affectation. So full of need.

. . .

One day at the bottom of the Wedgwood exit ramp, descending from I65 north at mile 81 at thirty miles per hour, then twenty, then ten, there was a skeletal, sun-baked man with white stubble covering his face and a trucker's cap, something green with a mesh back, a mesh screen to allow the heat from the stretched skin around his skull to dissipate instead of fester there against his head, his humid wet hair. Nashville gave him a nice breeze at the back of his scalp. He occupied precious real estate, too. There was a bridge nearby. The cops were less aggressive there than other places around town. It was a high-traffic, sought-after perch for sign-holders and the homeless: *Will Work For Food, Former Vet Needs Help, God Bless You God Bless You God Bless.*

His sign simply said: *I AM HUNGRY.*

That was Nashville: hungry. The sign-bearer seemed to always be there in one form or another. At every intersection, every corner. Every office building and studio down Music Row.

A few miles north of the man holding the *HUNGRY* sign was the Alternative Energy recycling plant where we took the majority of our wood chips to be recycled into mulch. The plant was right downtown and it was dusty and loud and smelled like wet wood and oil and decay. We stopped the dump truck at the little cubby hole toll booth and said: "Fourteen yards of chips," a clean load, or "Fourteen yards of mix," which meant there was some wood in the back, too, or some brush, or a tangle of poison ivy vines, and we arced the new Ford550 diesel around, opened the rear gate and carabineered it to the body of the truck, and then *beep beep beeped* our way back to the mountain. The earth movers paused in their moving long enough for us to push the electric button that hoisted the hydraulic dump bed,

115

long enough to let the material from the truck swish out onto the ground, long enough for us to jerk the truck forward to get the last remnants out of the bed while it was still raised and then long enough for us to depart. Then the movers reshaped the mountains into gobble-sized bites and fed the grinding machines.

That was our Nashville.

A few miles west of the man holding the HUNGRY sign is where we made most of our money, which is where most of the money spilled out of Nashville, a few arteries of wealth pulsing down highway 431 and 31 and 70, larger and larger houses sprouting from the rich veins, then razed, then built even larger.

Nashville was so hungry, so rhinestoned and honkytonked but by then mostly just for tourist dollars. Nashville was lunch counter sit-in stained and scarred by 1916 fires and 1998 tornadoes that wound their way between the skyscrapers and targeted all the downtown churches, ripping them down to their bones, ripping out trees from the Hermitage, some planted by Andrew Jackson himself. Then everything rebuilt. Replanted. Gentrified. Everywhere driving through a kind of resurrection, if only one had the faith to believe. Or the money.

I also drove past our jobsites. My brother and I had climbed into the tops of trees all over town, and we couldn't drive more than a few miles without passing a yard watered with our sweat. A treescape shaped by our chainsaws. Grounds cleared and reordered by our rakes and chipper.

It was a strange mark to leave on a town. A funny kind of fame.

But everything in Nashville looked so different at night. All the chainsaw dissonance of the day settled into a hot quiet evening, depending on where you lingered. I tended to drive past all of those job sites and all over a serene city. Wonderfully cooler when the sun went down. And I wanted so desperately for something to happen. Maybe I wanted the noise and violence of the work day to linger just a little bit more. I tried to pray some nights to fill the silence. For the city and for my parents and for my brother and sisters.

My brother was out doing his own prowling. Most nights he would go out with other tree workers, sometimes to the bars, sometimes to parties around town. One night he went to a party with Thomas and Kenny, both part of the tree crew. Thomas's cousin needed security guards for a high school kegger out in a field. My brother said "Sure, sounds like fun," and they all piled into a truck and found the party and pressed their way into the center of all those kids, maybe a hundred high-schoolers, and started to mingle and talk and drink. My brother and his friends volunteered to build the bonfire because they had a truck-bed full of chainsaws. They went to work, scrounging through the nearby woods for fallen limbs and dead trees, buzzing things into lengths easy enough to drag to the fire. Before long there was a mountain of wood, which they quickly ignited as the kids applauded, and the whole spirit of the place ratcheted up. The party was coming alive.

And then this skinny, dark-haired kid showed up and proclaimed himself some kind of bartender. He had boxes of liquor and wine and he was setting up a little table with plastic cups and a metal box where he intended to put all the money. He had the prices worked out and started charging people for drinks.

Which was fine with my brother because he was asking for and receiving free booze. He was one of the chaperones, after all, and the builder of the bonfire. And everything was fine until Kenny went for another drink, his fifth or sixth, but the bartender decided to start charging, which made the tree guys upset. Kenny shoved the kid and became his own bartender, but the kid had some kind of telescoping lead bludgeon up his sleeve, which he extended and whapped against Kenny's skull. Kenny went down hard. Face first. Out cold.

The party suspended. A hundred high-schoolers collectively sucked in their breath as Aaron and Thomas pounced on

117

the kid within seconds of the blow. Nothing to cause long-term injury or paralysis, but they definitely let him know he shouldn't have hit Kenny with a telescoping lead baton.

Kenny's head was cracked wide open. Blood had poured over his face and already dried, matted into his stringy receding hair. He got up and stumbled half-dazed to find his attacker who, upon discovery, he clobbered with a left, which was his famous hitting arm, and the kid went down again.

And then everything sort of exploded, as if a match had been thrown into a sea of gasoline. The stomped-down bartender had gone to get a shotgun, and then there was screaming, and then Thomas walked briskly up to the kid with the shotgun and said, "If you're gonna pull that trigger you better fucking do it," and he was close enough to grab the barrel of the gun, which he held firmly against his own chest, and as he walked the kid backwards he kept saying, "If you've got the balls to bring this thing out you better have the balls to pull the fucking trigger."

The kid didn't have the balls. And my brother and his friends had to leave quickly because Kenny was in bad shape. He was talking funny and couldn't focus. They bolted from north of town to the south because Thomas's dad was a veterinarian and had cat tranquilizer and a staple gun to stitch up horses. Thomas got the gun ready and then he and Kenny needled some tranquilizer into their veins and then Thomas put the gun to Kenny's head and pulled the trigger.

Kenny screamed but Aaron told him not to be a pussy, and then Thomas took the gun and punched a staple into his own chest, winced, then did it again, just to prove it wasn't that bad. Kenny forgot the pain and laughed hysterically, which emboldened Thomas to drop his pants, push his penis to the side and staple his scrotum to his leg. That's when Aaron told them they were all fucking nuts and left to sleep in the truck.

The morning came quickly. The sun poured through the truck's camper top and Aaron began to bake. The stink of gasoline had soaked into his clothes and hair and skin. He squinted into the light, moaned, and said if he had had a shotgun big enough he would have aimed it at the sun and had the balls to blow it clean out of the sky.

...

Boom. Town. Nash. Ville.

My dad was painting it and my brother and I were shaping its treescape. A fleeting imprint. The freshly pruned tree canopies became dense again after a few years. The branches started to criss and then cross. We had to sweep through another time. I would rediscover my tie-in points from years before and retrace my climb. Dad's paint would eventually peel. The walls would get punctured, need a fresh coat. And there was Dad with his brushes and buckets, day after day, spreading fresh color.

Someone told me the story of Sisyphus once, rolling his giant punitive rock up a hill for eternity only to have it slip his grip and roll down again and I said, "That's *our* story!"

One of our customers lived in a sprawling ranch house beneath the state's champion red oak, which we had ascended at least a dozen times over the years. There were a few oaks that measured a little bigger, somewhere out east, but this was considered one of the oldest. We had climbed it so many times trying to keep the tree healthy and our customers safe in its shadow. We had installed cables to keep house-side limbs secure in high winds and pruned the entire crown to allow wind to pass through more easily. We had scrupulously kept up with the deadwood and knew the tree as well as Sam Donald's, every fork and hollow and bend. We knew where the birds liked to build their nests. We had seen generations of birds hatch and take flight.

Despite our efforts the tree lost half its top in a storm. It crashed into the yard, leaving a terrifying half-tree that loomed over the house with a heavy lean. It would crush the entire structure if it were to come down. We chipped up the felled limbs and spent a long time simply sitting at the tree's trunk, which had the girth of an inflatable yard pool, talking through options. We considered burying a pillar in concrete deep in the front yard and running a cable into the top of the tree to support it. We talked about strategically reducing the height of the tree and training it further away from the house. Our customers weren't convinced. They had spent too many nights listening to the tree groan above them. They were scared as hell.

. . .

There is no single way to take down a tree. There are, in fact, a million variables. Some trees you simply approach, suck your thumb and thrust it into the air to get the direction of the wind, slice a notch, then a back-cut, and then the whole thing flops over with a giant rush of air and energy. If the tree is big enough you feel the ground tremble beneath your boots. This is a technique for fields, or in big yards, or in any situation where there's little or no danger that the tree could get cockeyed and kill something of value. But even an azalea is valuable so you have to be sure. God forbid you kill a boxwood or a rhododendron—it could wipe out your paycheck for a week.

Most of the time things get technical. As in you have to climb the tree and take it down piece by piece. It can be as easy as climbing up and cutting each limb, stripping the tree, airmailing the branches by allowing each limb to hinge down and fall close to the trunk as if the tree had a skirt you were dropping around its singular wooden ankle. This is standard with pines and other conically-shaped trees. But even then things can go wrong. If you drop a limb and the tip hits the ground first, that limb can bend and then bounce and sometimes it can get so much spring it will shoot off and kill something. Something you thought was safe. Kenny killed a screen door once. The Eagle Scout killed the windshield of a service van parked twenty feet from his tree. He should have checked his perimeter.

And then there is a real technical removal, which means each limb needs to be roped down individually, or somehow secured so nothing happens in an uncontrolled way. Everything must be precise. This when a tree has grown over a roof, or a deck, or a garage housing expensive imported automobiles.

Technical takedowns are elaborate works of engineering genius. A thousand choices, and each with serious, even deadly consequences. Every movement, every action is a negotiation with gravity, an ongoing conversation in which you ask a question—*Dear Gravity, I was wondering if this will happen that way if I do the following things*—and then you look around for some indicator, some sign from the invisible force pulling and pulling all around you, and perhaps you feel the wind blow softly in the direction you'd like to send a limb and you feel affirmed, so you tie your knots and think through each step of your choice, consider again all of the variables, and pull the cord on your chainsaw, which is something of a commitment.

Removals can be sad, too. There isn't a tree person alive, no matter how money-hungry or calloused of heart, who doesn't grieve over the destruction of some ancient oak, growing for a hundred years only to have a contractor erect a house in its shadow, and then, with the first strong wind, start getting a little nervous about all that wood swaying just above the brand new slate roof. Maybe at first the customers wanted the tree, considered hanging a swing from one of the lower branches, but then they realized the lowest branch weighs over two tons, and this is an organic thing and therefore unpredictable, and last night, when the winds came, they heard a fibrous moan.

Most tree people grieve even as they fill the gas tanks of their chainsaws. We always worked hard to save such trees, especially that champion half-oak, and to change the minds of people who suddenly consider themselves owners of all that ancient life, including asking customers to accept the inherent risk of living underneath these magnificent creations and know that the percentage chance of dying from a wind-felled tree or snapped limb are about the same as getting attacked by a hammerhead shark.

Of course our oak-tree customers didn't have to pass hammerhead sharks every time they went to the grocery store or sipped margaritas on the porch. They insisted. They wanted it down. This is how we did it:

My brother strapped his worn spikes to his feet, pulled his harness over his hips, checked all of his equipment and the three-foot bar on our Stihl 036, which was not our biggest saw but after some retrofits carried the most torque.

He got to the top of the oak quickly and found the most advantageous fork through which to run his climbing rope, because the angle mattered. The higher and more central, the easier and safer it would be as he maneuvered through what was left of the tree's canopy.

Now he was off his lanyard and attached to his climbing rope and he set about securing his lowering blocks from the strongest forks so when he cut sections of tree, a person on the ground gripping the other end of the bull rope could let them down safely. No dead azaleas, no dead slate roofs. A few more workers would be waiting to grab the tips of each limb as they were lowered in order to position the trunk-ends toward the chipper.

My brother quickly set about dismantling the tree, making his notch, tying a loop that cinched up like a slipknot under the weight of the branch, and then his final cut, hoping each limb would swing in the right direction, that the tips would clear the roof of the house, and that Kenny was still lucid and holding on to the rope's other end because it's likely he was up until four in the morning drunk, high, fist fighting. It was always possible he was asleep behind the tinted lenses of his safety glasses.

Aaron yelled "HEADACHE!" because it warned everyone that he was about to do something. Each time we all stopped and stared. It was the responsibility of every person on the ground to know what was happening above. If you got hit, it was your own fault, regardless of context or circumstance. We all scurried around on the ground that day trying our hardest to look as if we had everything under control and Aaron would cut through a new limb and the bull rope held by Kenny would cinch tight and the limb would lower successfully to the ground, where Thomas and the Eagle Scout and I untied it and dragged it to the chipper.

Eventually Aaron had cut and lowered everything but the trunk, and he was perched there at the top of a single, giant, totem-like stem of tree, which meant we were down to the crane work.

First he cut a goliath notch. He was careful where he threw the wedge because once the Eagle Scout had performed a flawless takedown on a tree that had grown up in the middle of a customer's deck, and when he got back to the trunk he cut a notch and let that slice of hardwood fall and then it bounced off the deck and smashed through an ancient, priceless, irreplaceable window leading into the customer's kitchen.

We all determined never to repeat his mistake and made sure to throw each discarded chunk onto the ground strategically and softly, holding our breath most times until it came finally to rest.

The red oak was so big that our crane was inadequate. We had to hire a company to come out with their giant industrial machine, and Aaron was doing his best to shout instructions at the operator who was used to craning up I-beams and lumber to construction sites.

The tree's circumference was so big that Aaron had to girdle it with his chainsaw and when he finally completed the circle, the crane lifted the sections away and placed them heavily onto the back of our truck. When all the sections were down Aaron placed his saw on the ground and removed all his gear, looking kind of defeated.

"Hell of thing," I said.

"I've got an idea," he said. "Let's take the trunk to the farm. We'll recycle it."

"Into what?" I asked.

"I'll figure it out," he said.

The section was about 12 feet long and the flare about the same in circumference. Once home, it was too heavy for the hydraulics on our dump truck to lift so we had to tie it to the hitch of another truck and drive each away from the other. It sat outside Aaron's cabin for weeks, then months. We thought about simply milling it but we wanted to honor it somehow, for surviving so long, for being sacrificed for the safety of a family who chose to live in its shadow.

One day Aaron said he had talked to a teacher at a local Waldorf school who wanted to build a unique playhouse at the school grounds. He thought about the trunk, and how it could be hollowed out to make a fairy-tale house. We could build a roof on top. Make little shuttered windows all around.

I should have learned my lesson from the cherry stump and my attempt at turning it into a chair. But I volunteered again, and took another of our big chainsaws outside and started plunge cutting. Red oak is dense and heavy and unforgiving. Aaron had achieved a fairly clean cut when he girdled the tree. I could see all those rings clearly at the very base, each one a remarkable year of life. The kickback from pushing the tip directly into the middle of all those rings was almost uncontrollable.

I worked on the trunk for a week in my spare time. Progress was slow and the tree stunk and the work was dangerous as hell. The further into the trunk I went the smaller the pieces I could remove. It was a game of angles. Once, I buzzed through the outside bark. I thought I was safely within the circumference but suddenly the bar punched through. I figured I would eventually turn the puncture into one of the windows.

I started to lose interest in the project but I was far enough in that we couldn't salvage the wood for anything other than the shell I was trying to create. The trunk just lay there. I visited it less and less. The teacher from the Waldorf academy stopped calling to check on our progress. Before long we rolled the trunk over by the cherry chair where it, too, went completely untouched and the weeds started growing up its sides and before long the deep gray bark was overwhelmed by green.

...

When we first started doing tree work there were only a few reputable companies in town. There were a handful of hackers who would descend from surrounding counties every time a storm came through, scavengers with big equipment, but we were one of the early companies who tried to stay up to date with best practices, read a little in the tree magazines, and remain on the cutting edge of modern arboriculture.

Nashville, meanwhile, was still booming. There was so much money. Wealth was pouring out of California, where $700k bought you a parking space, but people were building compounds in Nashville where the same money bought you a few acres and a mansion. And what do you do when you buy a mansion? You can't let it be flanked by scraggly trees full of deadwood and hazards. You hire real arborists, people who know about included bark and compartmentalization of pruning wounds and the biological negatives of topping trees.

You hire us. We were mangled but articulate. Even Kenny, although he was often told to stay in the truck when customers were around. We were sunburned and scarred and maybe sweating a little IPA from the previous night but we knew what was best for your trees and we would love them and care for them and climb them only occasionally pausing, only in the highest forks, to take in the view of the city which always seemed to sprawl below us, at our feet, out beyond the trunks of our trees.

From that vantage point we pruned downward. Trees are so wonderfully tiered. The work reflects this. You circle and circle, creating order from chaos as you go, earthbound orbiting while bringing space and light to thickets of branches, opening everything to the air and wind and moisture, sculpting and organizing and smoothing out the view.

I loved this part of the work: bringing my own sense of balance and order to the randomness of nature. Or rather, furthering the balance and order already there by helping the tree along its predetermined journey, be it multiple-leadered, single stemmed, heavily leaning or perfectly upright. I would come along and pluck out the idiosyncrasies like a plover in a crocodile's mouth. A robust symbiosis. Through pruning and deadwooding I would remove elements of decay and disease and future hazards, and in return I stayed strong, healthy, and relatively well-paid. $20 an hour, on my way to $25.

Most of my money went into a bank account earmarked for travel. I accumulated passport stamps, international phone cards, patches, journal entries, and what I had begun describing as deep cracks in my faith. It was hard to find the right language for the precise feeling.

I fell in love with a German woman on a train. A German woman on a bicycle. A Finnish woman at an orphanage and a Romanian woman while hitchiking. Pretty much in that order. I fell in love with the rhythm of trains. Living on cheese and bread and jam from my backpack. And park benches, which I first really discovered in Krakow, Poland: the wooden helms of the universe, the wrought iron centers of the cosmos. There were days when I lived, ate, and slept on the same bench without really moving.

I fell in love with the deep exhale of relief after navigating borders, border guards, late night baggage searches and conversations based on three or four shared words. *Hello. Goodbye. Thank you. I am hungry.*

I would enter BNA so large with my travels. Bigger than my city. Inflated to the point of bursting. Too vast and sophisticated for Nashville, I thought. Perhaps even for my faith.

Not long after I returned from Russia I came home and told my dad I was pretty sure I couldn't believe in Jesus anymore. Dad had been living in his duplex for a year and we were again on speaking terms. He had never stopped painting long enough to leave the country but he understood faith. Also its lack. I was reaching out.

He smiled. He said, "Josh, before you move on theologically or geographically, as in right now, before you take another step, you should repent. Just repent. Repent of your hubris and pseudo-intellectualism and your drunkenness on your own experience and repent of that list you keep of the countries you've traveled to and all those fragments from magazines and beer labels stuck in your journal and all of the things that make you feel special and important and different from others. Just repent. As much as you know you don't know shit."

I wish he would have put it that way. Those are my words. But the sentiment was all his, even though I can't remember exactly how he stated it—the mandate to step away from my own puffed up assuredness and admit I was tiny, my awareness was minuscule, and that perhaps there was still much I had yet to experience or understand, both about the world and my movement through it.

He was right. I knew it even before he said it. Part of what was so exciting in my tree-money-to-travel adventures was coming back to Nashville, which felt increasingly provincial, and swaggering through the city, back to the trees, feeling as if I had some privileged, esoteric angle on the planet. And my faith was wrapped up in it, along with the spiritual crises I collected from my trips. It was energizing to be conflicted. I was fueled by feeling fraught, especially launching from a city so galvanized in its evangelical certainties. Back then all the giant, opulent church facades seemed indistinguishable from the Sunday school felt boards of Love Inn, replete with their smiling Bible characters and simple promises of hope and healing. The world I had been exploring started to feel like a storm front moving over the facades, the felt going limp from hard rain, the fabric stretched taut from strong winds, tearing apart at the seams. Zacchaeus and his sycamore ripped away. Jesus flapping limply next to where the tree once stood.

I, meanwhile, was postured up like one of those contemporary country music stars on their album covers slapped onto bus benches all over Nashville, leaning against some urban landscape in denim and trucker cap looking pensive, furrow-browed.

I peered around thinking I could see everything for what it truly was. Dad came along and saw right through me.

...

Dad's tiny duplex sat just south of Nashville. He had been the first to leave the farm. He didn't take much with him, just a few loads of paint stuff in his minivan. He filled his new shed with all of his equipment and the rest spilled out around his back door. We had to walk through a corridor of junk to get inside. It was a cheap, two-bedroom deal and he slept in one room and set up his drum kit in the other. He said the neighbors didn't mind when he practiced, even though it rattled the whole house. He practiced all the time.

Dad's artistic vision was shifting, too, from walls slathered in faux finish to found objects and furniture, American flags made from strips of white and red cedar, fluted pedestals routered out and embedded with iron crosses, then sealed with thick polyurethane. He started peeling off the multi-colored paint crusted around the insides of some of his mixing buckets and framed the strips in gold, silver, sometimes reclaimed barn wood. He called the series "Art Jive." He started attending art shows and setting up his booths at the Opry Hotel and even made flyers for his new project, "Andersen Art and Associates."

He worked alone and I never asked him who his associates were, but I imagined him including the trinity in all he did, even to the point of giving Father, Son, and Holy Spirit a byline on his propaganda.

"Redemptive Art," he wrote of his work, "is my attempt to use existing or recycled materials, including other art pieces and combine them in larger context. A person or object is only elevated when impacted by a higher kingdom. (Except in the sub-molecular world when an atom is smashed!!)"

Dad's "About Me" statement said he had lived in Nashville since 1986, and "enjoyed the growth and recognition of our town as a center for arts and music of all descriptions."

Still booming. Still creeping outward toward Chattanooga, Louisville, Memphis to the west and Knoxville to the east. "I am even making tables and collectable artifacts from an actual 'Cedar of Lebanon' tree which was recycled from the estate of the late Minnie Pearl," he wrote. "How-Dee!"

Aaron and I were the ones who cut it down.

Aaron was the next to leave Sam Donald's farm. He moved his whole operation closer to the city. He used his crane to re-trace his construction steps, hammered out all the locust pegs that once held his cabin together, and placed the whole thing neatly on a trailer. He bought a beat up old house close to town with a big workshop and parked all the equipment out back. He punched a hole on the living room wall and installed his wood-burning stove. He reconstructed his twelve by twelve timber frame into what he started calling the Honeycomb Hideout in the back yard. He gathered there with the crew each morning to go over the day's agenda, dispersing print-outs of job orders and maps, talking through particular challenges of particular jobs and where to park which vehicles and where to set which ropes and where to grab lunch on the go. He knew that by eleven a.m. everyone was starving.

I would soon be gone, too. The farm's center had ceased to hold. We were all flung outward from the fields.

But Mom still clung to Sam Donald's farm. She dug in her heels and continued to live there with my baby sister, Danielle. Dad had started dating. Dad was a faux genius sitting around in bars talking to whoever would listen about his sponge tech-niques, his side tables, his hero Jesus Christ. Mom was still out in the field most days with her animals, sitting by the pond, no longer shaded by the red oak.

The turtles. The llamas and sheep. The Adirondack chair under the hackberry where she would preside over it all, still dreaming up improvements for the land, for her life there.

Nashville was forever booming. Mom sat there in the sun and waited and watched and felt the city shrapnel deep into Sam Donald's old fields.

Nine

I met my wife at a tree climbing competition I was busy losing. She crested a hill. That's the best way to put it: crested. She wasn't walking or strolling or shuffling as much as levitating toward me.

Although I was losing the day I had at least just won the aerial rescue event after successfully plucking the same old 170-pound dummy from a tree, lowering him safely to the ground. I was untying knots and recoiling rope when I saw her.

There she was. This woman. Cresting.

Maybe it was her cheeks. Something Scandinavian and pronounced and her eyes were the kind of blue that absorbs other blues—from a scarf, a shirt, the sky—and end up deepening in their own blueness.

She came to where I sat, a friend of the Eagle Scout's sister, there to support Jesse. So I told her my best tree-guy story, a story about how Kenny went to the bar one Friday, the week's wages in a fat cash roll in his pocket, and how when he left two guys followed him out to the parking lot, how a third rushed from the bushes just as it dawned on Kenny what was happening, and how Kenny was pretty fast in his work boots and made it to the back of his truck before the three strangers descended on him and how he had just enough time to grab the top-handled chainsaw he used in the trees and pull on the cord while stumbling back once, twice, and how the engine screamed to life as he brought the saw down on his attacker's collar bone full throttle, stopping the other two strangers in their tracks.

My wife cringed but wanted more. I told her how Kenny meticulously cleaned his saw the next day, dismantling the whole thing as if it were a precision rifle, scrubbing, oiling, spit-shining all the parts. How he kept looking over his shoulder for weeks afterward.

We had lots of those stories. I suddenly wanted to tell her

all of them, to bring her as close to my world as I could, let her see everything, even though I had known her for ten minutes.

She listened and seemed to care. She said her name was Kathryn and that she was in school, double majoring and double minoring, Spanish and literature and law and international studies.

"I travel!" I said. "I mean, internationally."

But right then, having just won the aerial rescue event, I wanted her to know I was a tree guy, tethered to a world of danger and testosterone and almost death all the time. That when a felled tree hit the ground, and if we couldn't reach it with the crane, the crew and I would attack it like termites, chainsaw-buzzing the wood into pieces small enough to lift by hand. I wanted her to know that the guy recently grunting next to me every day was Craig, a full-time tree man and part-time comic whose jokes often involved crack whores, who smoked forty cigarettes every 24 hours and who once caught the tip of his chainsaw on a burl, and I wanted her to know how the machine kicked back like a sprung catapult and how the chain chomped into the flesh of his right shoulder which severed his tattoo in half, the one with angel wings attached to a heart with the name of his on-again-off-again wife written in cursive at the center: *Chris / tine*.

She said she was on her way to Spain, would be gone for a year. I wanted to tell her I could go with her, that I could make enough money, that maybe I could try and be a good Christian and save the world from over there. *Where? Salamanca? Sure, from over there.*

Instead I told her how the Eagle Scout made finger puppets out of the skins of small rodents and scared the girls at high school, how sometimes when we reached the trunk flare of a felled tree it needed to be quartered, so the axes came out, the eight-pound splitting mauls whose presence seemed to amp everyone up and the shirts came off and you could see the deep red burns of neck and arms contrasted against milk-white torsos, the menacing heavy metal tattoos, the crisscross of scars, and how we circled the slabs eye-balling the ones we thought we could split, hurling ourselves at our target, the growth rings a kind of bull's eye, slamming the steel head of the axe into the freshly exposed flesh of the tree. Against the grain. Find the cracks. Hit hard.

"And music," she said. "My dad's a kind of musician. A Christian musician."

Music! Faith! I told her about Mudpan Melvin, and how my brother and I could have gone into faux painting, too, but how instead we did this thing, this totally unique labor called tree work, and we could footlock up ropes using a *Prusik* loop that would bind from our weight if we fell, and how sometimes we footlocked without the knot, no safety, and how if we slipped without a *Prusik* we could plummet to our death and burn the prints off our palms trying to stop the fall.

"So how are you doing?" she said, meaning in the competition.

"Pretty good," I said. "My brother's always the one to beat."

We looked up simultaneously. I took it as a sign. My brother was soaring through a tree's canopy in record time, ringing bells as he went from station to station. I realized more than anything I wanted to introduce her to Aaron.

Love, then, was inextricably linked to vocation. After the competition, my first date with my future wife was to a tree removal. It was a weekend job, something for extra money. The customers wanted a better view of the lake from their back deck. They wanted someone to mow a swath through a stand of lanky, tall hardwoods so they could see the water.

Alan Jackson lived on the other side of the lake. "He did it too," they said. If the local country music star (most wealthy Nashville neighborhoods had at least one) said it was cool, the case was closed. I didn't argue.

Kathryn read C.S. Lewis's *Space Trilogy* from the deck as I climbed up and down, up and down, lopping off ten-foot sections of crown at a time.

"How's the view?" I yelled.

"I can see the water!" she yelled back.

And this was our genesis. So I wrote her a letter, once, try-ing to explain the feeling of it all. What it was really like. An arboreal love letter in second person trying to bring her into the same tree canopies as me.

A month in the trees and you know things, I wrote. You know how to back a chipper down a winding driveway with-out jackknifing the machine, how to sharpen a chainsaw until it cuts through hardwood as if it were tofu—one tooth at a time, steady and methodical on your knees with a round file, then a flat file for the rakers to ensure everything bites.

I explained how you tie your lowering block right below a high notch and run your bull rope through the pulley. How you tie a running bowline knot—a little mechanical miracle—around the section of tree above you.

You take a deep breath, I wrote. Test all the ropes, the pul-ley, your own lanyard. You look at the ground and yell *HEAD-ACHE!* The crew will quickly snap to attention.

Kenny will mumble something about tortilla chips as he wraps the bull rope around a lowering device at the base of the tree and then you unclip your chainsaw from your harness and pull the cord to bring it to life. Please beware, I wrote. Things just got exponentially more dangerous. You'll never be sure of the actual percentages, but you figure that the chance you could die has to be at least six times greater than before that chainsaw woke up. You are so alert and alive and you whisper something sweet to the gravity pulling around you and tell Kenny to let the rope "run" a little, which will keep the section from hinging over and slamming directly back into the trunk, which would give you a ride every bit as violent as a mechanical bull in a honky-tonk bar.

You level the chainsaw against the flesh of the tree, an inch or two above the bottom of the notch, which is opening like the smile of the Cheshire Cat in front of you. You squeeze the trigger and hold steady. The chainsaw growls and then bites.

If you've done anything wrong at this point it's too late, I wrote. All you can do is hope that your negotiation with gravity went well, that your sweet nothings were well received, that you asked the right questions and received the right answers and mostly that Kenny is still conscious.

He is. He lets the rope run a little as the piece comes swinging, which allows the wood to lose much of its momentum from the fall and it gently taps against the trunk further down. You still feel it but not much. You should plan on buying Kenny a beer at lunch. He's undoubtedly thirsty.

If everything goes well, you will be finished and you'll step away from the remaining bone of tree onto solid dirt, let your harness slip past your hips and jangle to the ground. And even though you might stop listening, I wrote, gravity still has much to say.

...

My wife helped me pack my things at Sam Donald's farm, all of which fit into the bed of a 1980 Toyota pickup truck named Gwendolyn, and helped me sort through the paperwork of starting college at a small liberal arts school outside of Philadelphia. Although I never finished high school, I had decided that, at twenty-six, I wanted to build efficient, streamlined bakeries all over the Global South so churches could start food ministries—something tangible, real, sustaining—instead of trying to run around saving souls. I was going to model it after a bakery I ran in Albania. I figured a degree in nonprofit management was what I needed. Or, I don't know, anthropology. Something international and others-focused. My wife was a good academic influence.

"You need homework," she said once over dinner. "You should go to college for deadlines and grades."

She might have been thinking of my normal context for intellectual discourse, which was the tree crew, all of whom comprised my inner circle. The Eagle Scout. Craig the Comic. Kenny, Thomas, my brother. They were all smart, and spent their days doing things very few people either would choose to do or be physically able to do, but I kept running around trying to conduct amateur international relations conversations without knowing it was a real discipline, theological exegesis with people whose only relationship to Jesus was as an expletive, and half-economic, half-humanitarian dialogues with friends who simply wanted to drink their beers in peace. Kathryn knew I needed some scaffolding around what was becoming a loose-cannon, misfired intellectualism.

So we drove north for a routine admissions meeting at the school that seemed like the best fit and ended up having a serendipitous run-in with the president of the university, who was kind enough to ask me about myself, and when I got to the Love Inn part he laughed, and when I got to the Russian orphanage part he wept, and when I got to the tree part he offered me his on-the-spot "Presidential Scholarship," the first of its kind, an opportunity to take care of the trees on campus in exchange for a full academic ride.

"Twelve hours of work a week and you've got a bachelor's degree in four years," he said.

"I can slip on my boots right after class," I said. "Will the professors be angry if I smell like gas and chipped wood?"

We shook hands. The whole thing felt divine.

Kathryn helped me study astronomy, helped me through the math parts. She quizzed me for anthropology tests and helped me pronounce my Spanish vocabulary. I began reordering the tree lines of campus between classes.

Kathryn was also understanding when I realized that non-profit management would kill my soul, and what I really wanted was a degree in journalism and writing, based on my experience in Russia and now in workshops, which felt like these brief, communal portals opening up into the human experience. Wonderful, life-giving conversations not just on craft, but what it means to be sentient and alive.

She never rolled her eyes when I said such things, pretty much verbatim, but instead advised me to run with it, see where it might lead. A professor had suggested I write about trees. For a while, I scribbled about nothing else.

Kathryn found a job at a philanthropic investment firm close to campus, an organization helping rich people give their money away to programs that wouldn't squander it. Kind of like a traditional investment firm except the return was not monetary but *life change*.

And then one day I asked her to marry me. The thought had been percolating for a long time, and we both knew it made sense, but maybe I was still shell-shocked from my parents' divorce, and maybe we were both a little cynical of the institution, having seen it dissolve so many times. But I had a ring, my grandmother's ring given to me by my mother, and one day we were walking down the street to our little church having a difficult conversation about the future and us in it, us together, and we walked into the little church's lobby only to walk right through it, back outside to a bench made from a slab of cedar sitting by a busy road. She was crying and I was crying. We had been together long enough to have slipped into seasons of pure survival, lots of ups and downs, almost-leavings and returns. We both felt like we had eyes wide open about this marriage thing. We felt like we knew what we'd be signing up for.

And then a friend crossed the street on his way to church and said, "I see you're both sitting on the bench of indecision."

We quickly wiped tears from our eyes.

"The what?" I asked.

"The bench of indecision," he said again, by which he meant the place where some parishioners would sit trying to decide whether they should go to church that morning or to the café across the street for a latte, but we read deeper significance into his words, felt it hit harder than he meant it, and after he passed by I asked my wife to wait, just sit still, as I ran top speed back to our house, grabbed my grandmother's engagement ring, and breathlessly back to the bench of indecision where, amidst even more tears, we decided to decide.

...

We got married thirteen days after our bench of indecision decision. We called all of our immediate family and closest friends, apologized for the short notice, but suggested that if they could make it, we'd in turn try and make it worth their while. We were at a stage of life when it seemed as if everyone we had ever known was getting married, and we were facing a summer filled with a dozen ceremonies, so we said let's get this done. We called in favors, borrowed chairs and tables from my university, pulled off a ceremony in the middle of campus right under trees I had been tending for three years, and catered Indian food in our back yard for a reception. All of our Philly friends came, our Nashville family, too. My brother stood next to me, the Eagle Scout next to him, my baby sister Danielle next to him.

It was one of the best days of our lives. So simple, lovely, concrete. It was a turning point. A stake in the ground around which we would both pivot. I was leaving my trees, leaving my college. We would be living in southern Mexico within a year. Everything whizzing by so fast but then there are days that feel like imprints, the images crisp around the edges, seared into your memory.

I still see her that day. Kathryn in her elegant borrowed dress, a combined look of exultation and awe and embarrassment as she descended the outdoor stairs for the ceremony. My eyes filled with tears, joy knotted in my throat, a deep sigh as she reached me there at our makeshift altar. I see my brother in his wrinkled linen, remember the pre-ceremony tequila, the endless arm wrestling. I see my parents, an awkward binary clumsily circling, and the swirl of excitement and alcohol and anticipation that led my wife and I exhausted to our room that night, to each other's arms, to the first waning hours of what we promised each other would be forever.

...

After we were married Kathryn and I quickly started piecing together our plans for Mexico, deciding at last on Oaxaca as our temporary home, a place to play with words in two languages, a place to begin understanding—practicing, daily—what it meant to be married.

We stayed only a few blocks from the city's center where we would walk every day, the famous *zócolo*, finding park benches on which to linger and watch the surges of activity from morning until night, and I would trace the lines of the giant laurel trees with my eyes, imagining what it would feel like to climb them, especially the *laurel de los conciertos,* the tree of concerts, of music, whose canopy had hung over the production of a million notes. I imagined it still rustling with the remnants of all those songs.

I thought this way a lot in Oaxaca. Looking everywhere for meaning and words to get at the center of that meaning. Mostly I failed. My Spanish was infantile and my writing in English seemed so clunky it could never paint a proper portrait of what I was seeing and feeling and wanting to describe.

One day we decided to head east out of Oaxaca City to the "unremarkable" village of El Tule, according to our guide book, a standard pueblo with a church, a market, lots of fruit. The only thing that distinguished El Tule was a tree. But it was a very big tree. In fact, it was said to be the largest single biomass on the planet, although I wasn't sure how anyone could possibly gauge such things, all those sequoias tickling the clouds in California, the seas of aspen forest whose roots wind together for miles underground.

The specifics didn't really matter. For me, a person whose

relationship with trees had been more intimate than most, it felt like something of a pilgrimage, a journey to the center of the tree-person's universe, a homecoming for my wandering tree-boy's heart.

And it was a little embarrassing, but pulling up to our bus stop and seeing the giant green canopy dwarfing the church next to which it had been growing for a few thousand years was making me giddy. I was yanking on Kathryn's arm, pulling her along the sidewalk like a child on a toy store mission.

"That tree's no joke," I said, smiling, squinting from across the street and struggling to speak with the eloquence I felt the tree deserved. "That's the real deal."

I talked as if other trees I had known had suddenly become facsimiles, mere seedlings from this, the mother tree, the Mecca tree, the fulcrum tree around which all other trees bent and swayed in their respective breezes.

It was gargantuan. For three pesos each we were allowed to circle the thing, a long walk indeed, staring at its enormousness from every angle except (I felt the urge to climb it like an addict in a supermarket full of fixes) from above. I was in awe. I had never seen such a structure, its enormous root flares like the flying buttresses of Notre Dame, its branches tangling into the sky like the muscled arms of a storybook kraken. It was so big. All my words for enormous short-circuited.

And despite its size—58 meters of girth and 42 meters of height—such delicacy. Its fernlike, soft branches swept almost to the ground, down to my fingertips, extending all the way past the iron fence to the street to greet even those who couldn't afford the three-peso admission. What a tree, I thought as I touched the tips of its branches with my fingers. Benevolent, kind, accommodating. This was the best tree in the world.

But I had secret thoughts that I couldn't quell. Ones that, if they could be seen on a screen, would probably have gotten me exiled from El Tule. Perhaps all of Mexico. I had already begun cutting the tree down in my mind, choosing the best leverage points for removing its immense branches, imagining the entire thing as a scaffolding from which I could dismantle the world's largest single biomass, limb by giant limb. I wanted to call my brother.

This was part of the sickness of our vocation. Having pruned a thousand trees and removed just as many, it was easy to view them merely as challenges, problems to be solved, paychecks. I still pruned the trees in the medians of highways as I whizzed by.

But El Tule came with warnings. The green iron fence keeping me a safe distance from its trunk was hung with signs that said in multiple languages, "Please don't cut my branches. I am a living thing." German, English, Spanish. It's as if they were hung there just for me. It's as if they knew my past. I could feel the icy stares of the *policía turísticas* on my back, imagined they could see who I was by the scars on my forearms, the dried tree blood from back home still crusted into my jeans.

"I'm sorry," I said to the tree, penitently, a declaration of guilt in the church yard to a different kind of confessor. "I had bills to pay."

. . .

By the time my wife and I reached El Tule in Oaxaca I had racked up quite a record of the "world's largest." I had seen the largest bronze doors in the world—7.5 tons each, twenty-four feet high, twelve inches thick. They lived in Nashville attached to a replica of the Parthenon.

I had seen what at the time was the largest cross in the western hemisphere, rocketing 19 stories into the sky on the outskirts of Amarillo, Texas in a town called Groom (Last I checked it had been eclipsed by a cross in Illinois eight feet higher).

And although I never stopped, I had seen billboards for the largest groundhog in the world. The interstate signs were some of the precious little scenery dotting the Kansas countryside. The friends who stopped were disappointed to find that the animal was not, in fact, living, but only a shabby replica of a groundhog, constructed of plaster and chicken wire.

The tree of El Tule, however, was definitely alive. It was said to be two thousand years old, which meant it was already photosynthesizing when Jesus was hanging limp and broken on his own tree. Of course it was two thousand years old *más o menos*, "more or less," which, like many things in Mexico, meant its age was open to interpretation. "I'll get there at 6 p.m." (*más o menos*), meant sometime before 8. "It'll take you an hour" (*más o menos*), meant more than two but probably less than four.

Yet even with a few more or a few less years, the thing was ancient. Older than New York City or the Liberty Bell or anything else I could think of in the States, either organic or constructed. And what was astounding beyond the tree's size and age was all the life that existed outside of its own vascular system. All the birds nesting in the peels of its bark, and the bees, too. The tree of El Tule was loud—so much life swarming and perched around its canopy. There were various mosses growing parasitically from its limbs and then there were all of us people, circling its trunk like planets around a sun, snapping pictures and gawking. The tree was indeed a universe, buzzing with energy and life, dying and regenerating and creating its own gravitational pull around which so many living things, including my wife and me, gratefully orbited.

It was busier than usual that day. We had come during *Semana Santa*, the holiest of Mexican holidays and perhaps the second most popular right behind *Navidad*—a time when vacationers bottle-neck through the streets and into the famous cathedrals of Oaxaca. The church of El Tule, too, was bustling with worshipers and pilgrims and tourists from Austria and Ohio. There was a woman on her knees in front of a plastic statue of Christ, thorns tearing open his flesh and blood trickling into his eyes. She was praying with real fervency, crossing herself, pressing her small dark hand to her lips and rocking back and forth. Walking past her with a grin was a man wearing a cowboy hat, the kind they sell to tourists back in the central market. His camera dangled from one hand—his fingers working the cord like prayer beads—and with the other he pointed out saints and flowers and paintings to his wife with a big, sincere smile.

This was one of the dramas of the modern state of Oaxaca. Places of piety, of beauty, all did double duty there. There were different plays being acted out on the same stages, the plots of which, at times, tenuously intersected. Some had come to that place to worship and pray, while others had come to look at a tree and take pictures. Still others, the entrepreneurs, had recognized both pilgrimages and set up shop, selling crucifixes made of palm fronds to the faithful and silk-screened t-shirts to tourists.

I suppose we were all looking for something. Some of us wanted to be wowed and awed, to see big things and take their pictures. Some wanted to make a living, to take advantage of the big-thing-seekers and put food on the table. And others wanted to connect to an invisible God through plastic stand-ins, to make sense of our world by placing control of it in the pierced hands of a God-man who knows what it is to suffer.

We had all come to the same place that day, all gathered together under the broad canopy of El Tule, its dappled shadow pouring without discrimination over the church and the hawkers and the tourists. Over my wife and I. The complex social buzz of *Semana Santa* mixed with the bees nesting in the bark. Women prayed. Cameras flashed. Children rejoiced as their fathers made another sale and somewhere in the highest limbs of the tree, a chorus ran unabated in the bellies of the birds.

I kept trying to explain to my wife how I felt, how my brother might feel, how amazing it was to be there with her. My enthusiasm was so great it began ushering me into conversations with those around me, with the woman and her young son who stood by me at the base of the tree. I asked her what she thought of the giant thing. After hearing the inarticulate mess that came out of my mouth she paused, smiled, and said in English: "It's beautiful. It's big. It's old."

...

Kathryn and I arrived in Oaxaca without an apartment, without any leads, collectively blind. We had a glossy map of the city we had picked up at the bus station and a few phone numbers of friends of friends. A backpack each. A bottle of water. Change in our pockets for a taxi and a beer.

We spent a few days walking the city, getting a feel for things and knocking on all the doors with more than a few electric meters outside, thinking that our best bet for an affordable apartment would be the ones that were unadvertised, the word-of-mouth kind of thing, the *I think I heard so-and-so had a place just around the corner* kind of thing.

It worked. We walked into a yoga studio and asked the woman behind the counter if she knew of an apartment for rent. We weren't sure why we chose it. It just looked nice inside, the kind of place we might sit down for coffee and a long talk about our future. When we asked about an apartment the woman's face blossomed immediately into a smile. She quickly closed up her studio and walked us the five blocks to her ancient colonial compound, on top of which sat a tiny concrete apartment with a view of a jacaranda tree, a church, and the fiery Oaxacan mountains. It was perfect. $250 a month, utilities included.

I hung some Christmas lights outside on the balcony. We filled the fridge with avocados and tortillas. We shoved pictures of our friends and family into the corners of our mirror so we could remember our people every time we combed our hair or adjusted our clothes.

It was a nice life up there. *Tranquilo y sencillo*. We triple washed our vegetables and fell asleep to the hum of a fan called "Cyclone." When I woke up in the morning I could see crumbs animated and crawling along our floors, bits of food cooperatively levitated along the ground by a column of ambitious ants. I loved those ants and their ingenuity. Together we were a make-shift community, symbiotic and hungry.

We hung flowers from the corrugated tin roof. They quickly turned dry and brittle. It didn't take long in the heat and sun. It seemed to make them even more beautiful. We found a guitar, too. Its in-tuneness fluctuated with the day's temperature but we didn't mind. We had a TV to watch *telenovelas* and a hummingbird that hovered outside our window for a few moments every day.

And from our roof, on clear days, I could see the giant jaca-randa tree waving its silvery arms at the nearby church, a wild conductor doing its best to direct all the music inside. They were everywhere in southern Mexico. Imported from Australia long ago. Spread around by the birds and wind and on the soles of so many people ambling by. They seemed to blossom eternally. Purplepink. We could lay in bed and watch birds resting in its branches.

One night, as we were preparing to return home, Kathryn came out with a pillow and held it up to the moonlight, showing a black and white moth perched there its true desire. She blew on its delicate wings and the moth scrambled for the light and then both my wife and insect were satisfied.

And that night I could see the mountains past our resident cell phone tower because the moon was so brilliant, and I could see the giant cross of Christ planted at a peak, blossoming from the cracked dirt, a long crisscross shadow even at night, like an angular finger pointing over the scrub brush at all the rick-ety shacks multiplying up the hill like cells. The poor had been pushed to the periphery in Oaxaca City and were building their way up the mountains at impossible angles because there was nowhere else to go. Instead of ceasing to hold, the center had simply priced them out. The roads were all dirt up there and the electric wires sagged like half-smiles. Residents had made it almost all the way up to the cross where there was a little bit of level ground and a breeze and I imagined that for some, finally

145

cresting that hill might feel like something of a prize. An arrival.

I couldn't stop thinking about time on that rooftop, and how in Oaxaca it seemed to crumple like a page. We walked from one edge to the other, wondering what happened to all the stuff in between. For the first time since I was a little boy reading beneath bedsheets with a flashlight at night, I remembered the illustration of a tesseract from a paperback copy of Madeleine L'Engle's beloved monomyth featuring a girl named Meg. A string stretched taut between two fingers, an ant journeying from one to the other, suddenly stepping easily—and quickly— across the gap when the fingers came together.

It fit our experience perfectly being freshly married in a new country looking for words. I thought of street *tlayudas* and El Tule and a long stream of conversations broken and frustrated and how suddenly it was almost time to go. Blurred and warped by its own rapidity. Five months had vanished and we were on our rooftop underneath the jacaranda tree and Christmas lights with our heads spinning, thinking of packing up and leaving, needing a new suitcase for all the gifts we had bought for friends and family.

And I remember that night feeling the same way about our lives, how our experiences—now just memories—were already settled into a deep canyon over which we had just gingerly stepped. I looked down and saw my brother and I racing down a rooftop, the first ascent of a sycamore, my wife cresting a hill at a competition. Kathryn looked down and saw the flea markets where her family once sold shoes, a basketball game where she blindly threw the ball backwards over her head, eyes completely closed, and sunk it for two remarkable points. Her coach told her to never pull a stunt like that again.

And in the darker crevices, the jagged places, we saw the memories that turned us from children into adults, into people who stagger a little under the world's weight—the time I went to Auschwitz and wanted to give up on God; the time Kathryn's friend Haylie walked out of a 27-story hotel window to be closer to Him.

I knew that night we would feel the same way in thirty, forty years, sitting on a different roof somewhere, trying in vain to remember which stars belong to which constellations. The canyon will have grown deeper and we will again wonder how we were able to step over its expanse so quickly.

That night my wife and I stepped from the edge of one furrowed page to the next and looked around, a little lost, asking for directions. I still sent my queries to the sky, generally, which in Mexico had been brilliant, the stars vivid like shot-gunned flecks of light, the sun brutal like close-by fire. If any directions descended while we were there I can't say, but they may have been muddled by the snarl of traffic and commerce on the streets that surrounded us. And I think we were okay with that. There was a broken kind of beauty down there, too.

Ten

The best tree climber in the world was for many years a small, dreadlocked German named Bernd "Beddes" Strasser. He was the best because he trounced all of his competitors at eight almost-consecutive international tree-climbing championships, beating the arboreal world's most aggressive and athletically absurd climbers. Of course, few people were actually watching, but those who *were* craned their necks in disbelief, awestruck at the fluidity, balance, and speed of a little wiry man climbing through tree canopies as if he had transcended the limitations of his own body.

I was watching, too, taking notes, doing my best to mimic his moves in my own less-than-world-class climbing career. Yes, I finally took the Tennessee championship from my brother one year, went on to land third at regionals—which won me a chainsaw—but I simply never had Strasser's prowess, his sixth climbing sense, which might just have been pure lunacy. He climbed as if he had talons and a tail.

Strasser never knew it, but I viewed him as something of a multi-faceted golden ticket. There was his climbing, which could transform any competitor into a champion if emulated properly. But there was also his story, his compelling, obscure, hitherto-unknown life story: the seed picking company he started to help scientific researchers gather specimens from the tippy-tops of impossible-to-reach trees, his innovations in tree climbing equipment and safety (he invented a widely used friction knot called the *Schwabisch*, named after a forest close to his home in Germany, the same knot that kept my brother and me alive day after day), his environmental advocacy and the fact that his weathered face and dreadlocks and charming smile seemed destined to grace the cover of *Outside Magazine, Men's Journal,* maybe even *GQ*. The dude was just beautiful.

I was sure I would be the one to break him into the media's

limelight, and at the same time catapult my fledgling writing career into the literary stratosphere. I was moving from college to a graduate writing program and was looking for stories. How many writers could follow him through the trees, after all? Who else could shove a microphone in Strasser's face two hundred feet up a tulip poplar and translate all that climbing jargon into palatable prose?

I was sure it was me. The right guy at the right time. So I emailed him. I explained my plan, called myself a "freelance writer," told him I'd like to do a feature profile that could almost definitely be shopped over to a top-tier glossy magazine with success. It took a while, maybe three months, but he eventually emailed back. Sounds good, he wrote,

> In the begin of july I will be in sequoia national park climbing mammut trees. It is within a project of the Berkley University of San Francisco.
>
> By the way, I was there last year already…these trees are incredible and sure enough they would be an amazing scenery for pictures…
>
> Happy days, climb safe
> Beddes

By the time I reached the last sentence, I had thrice imagined my byline on the cover of *ESPN Magazine*.

I made plans, consulted the atlas, realized that my wife could fly to her Thailand summer graduate program from out west, that I could drop her off in Seattle. I told my tree-climbing friends all about my summer project and started strength training so I could climb to three hundred feet without wheezing like a deflating tire. I told all my writing friends about the profile and heard a resounding chorus of: *Yes, you are the one to write this article—please remember us when you win the Pulitzer.*

And then we were off, all the way from my graduate program in coastal North Carolina to the West with a trunk full of journalism and climbing gear. Fresh batteries for the recorder. A brand new length of rope with which to tie a *Schwabisch* in front of the inventor himself.

But Strasser had been vague about the exact location and dates of his tree foraging in California. Early July, yes. Sequoia National Park, yes—but nothing more. I had emailed him a few times before I left, but still hadn't heard back with specifics. And yet I was committed, inching along our mapped-out route and waiting anxiously, daily, for Strasser's reply.

It never came. My wife and I sat roadside on the New Mexico/Arizona border wondering whether or not we could simply drive to the 202,430-acre park and find him in the trees.

"It would be like finding a monkey in a jungle," said my wife.

"Like finding a *Hyla arborea* tree frog in a rainforest," I said, always one to strain a metaphor.

Such is life. We secure something, lock it down, tether it to a tree only to see it drift away. Our plans and dreams and visions for the future, as sincerely as we make them, have a way of dismantling around us quickly, sometimes even as they are being constructed.

So we flexed. Hit a dead end, hinged, sought a new direction.

It was simple enough. Our tattered map came back out and we made new plans. We were only a half-day's drive from Grandma and Grandpa Andersen's retirement mecca down in Mesa, Arizona. My dad's mom and dad were both in their mid-nineties and, we figured, would be happy to have us. After that, we could continue up the coast, all the way to Seattle so Kathryn could catch her flight. From there, I thought I might even head back over to Rhode Island, where that year's International Tree Climbing Championship would be held, to track down Strasser and get my career-defining article after all. We pointed the

Civic westward and hit the gas, then south, and before long we started to see palm trees sprouting from the dry, fissured earth. We hardly looked back.

. . .

Marvin and Mildred Andersen, hunkered down as they were in Sioux City, Iowa during the fifties and sixties, had a lot to worry about. There was the ready-to-strike Red Army, the encroaching hippies with their noodle-arm dancing and gleaming eyes, the merciless, muscular Iowa winters that threatened, year after year, to freeze the pipes or slide Marv and Mil into ditches.

Life was downright scary. Then came the day Marv and Mil woke up to discover that their Afro-haired youngest son, Terry (wearing leather bellbottoms and munching on psyche-delic mushrooms), had left Iowa to become a drummer in San Francisco. And to make matters worse, their eldest son, Gary, was prowling around the Midwest in a motorcycle gang, beating up hippies who looked much like his little brother.

There wasn't much Marv and Mil could do. They sat in their single-story ranch house and realized that all the shifting cultural and political currents of the day had washed into their living room and swept away their family. And as time went on, things got even worse.

Terry went to jail for failing to show up at an Army base and got "born again" in his cell. He was a deserter but then he was found. When he was released, he ran off to play drums for Jesus at an Upstate Christian commune. At that point, Love Inn was almost as famous as Chicago's Jesus People USA. God's fisher-men were everywhere casting their nets wide and the fish were filling the boats to capacity.

Gary eventually traded his leather jacket for a navy uniform and started flying into the eyes of storms over Southeast Asia. Very scary stuff—one son living communally in an old dairy barn full of people with long hair, feeding himself from donations placed in something called the "Love Bucket," and the other careening his way into the middle of hurricanes in a rickety fuselage filled with jet fuel, with nothing but twenty thousand-feet of air and hungry sharks below.

The next generation wasn't much better. Marv and Mil proceeded to watch with a kind of open-mouthed awe as their son, Terry, got married and produced grandkids who grew into teenagers, joined Dagger gangs and went to juvenile detention and chose to attend Grateful Dead concerts instead of high school.

Of course Marv had dropped out of school, too, when he was only fourteen, but that was because his dad, Harry, had been killed by a pulley falling onto his head from the ceiling of the Sioux Tools Company. Marv had no choice but to end his education and go to work to cover the bills for his mom and four siblings. He just wasn't sure why his grandkids would choose to leave school to go see concerts.

What made perfect sense to Marv and Mil was the concept of working hard and diligently until one reached a well-deserved retirement. At that point, one would buy a motor home, quickly leave the Midwest in search of the perfect sun-drenched, communist-free compound in which to play golf deep into old age. A sanctuary. A Shangri-La. One would be especially lucky to discover an affordable place with a gate and an on-duty guard.

They did just fine. Marv and Mil bought a Winnebago and drove to California, visiting old true-blue American friends along the way and, although they had planned to drive all the way to Florida before making a final retirement decision, they hit Mesa, Arizona and stuck. Such heat! Such sunshine! Year-round golf and sprawling breakfast buffets!

They sold their Winnebago and built a small, adobe-lathered, air-conditioned house in Leisure World—a square mile compound filled with similar-minded retirees devoted to golf, woodshop, and buying stock in Wal-Mart.

They simply didn't know what to say when their nineteen-year-old grandson came to visit and told them, flippantly and with confidence, that retirement was a disease.

...

It's just that I was young and fired up. I was a freshly minted progressive Christian born again in a Nashville Waffle House. I'd been thinking a lot about the things in life that make us timid, fearful, and all the ways we sequester ourselves from others who are not like us. I couldn't stop thinking about how we Americans invest so much energy into living small, nervous, inconsequential suburban lives only to retreat into a kind of self-indulgent rest the second we actually get wise enough to make a difference.

By "a difference" I meant in the world, in an activist sense, as in people should go to their graves trying to make the planet a more just, equitable, safe and happy place. It was during the season when, slipping easily into a social justice reading of Scripture, I was basically the redux version of my dad, Terry, channeling my own neo-hippy energy into trying to save the planet instead of blast away from it to heaven. Instead of an Afro I had dreadlocks. In addition to the Bible I read Marx.

I still feel bad about that diagnosis. After all Marv and Mil's hard work and sacrifice, I came along and told them that everything they had ever worked for was pointless, fleeting, toxic. Then I slapped some sunscreen on my face and drove their golf cart to the pool. By the time I got back, Grandpa was on his third beer and had grilled me a cheeseburger. I'm not even sure he remembered my saying it. His was a thick skin and a short memory.

...

My grandparents had lived in Leisure World since 1987, a year after my family moved from Freeville to Nashville. I made my initial visit to Mesa when I was thirteen. At that age, before my idealism and some movies turned me into a Christian-y

Che Guevara, the compound was simply a marvel. It was like a theme park, a walled-in Disneyland where blue-haired people drove around manicured streets in tiny electric cars. I could go to the pool or play ping pong or pick grapefruits straight from Marv and Mil's back yard. Jackrabbits bounded over the gravel in the shadows of grackles.

It was pure magic: the giant globe at the front entrance; the twelve-foot walls stretching around an entire square mile; the fact that there was a real gate and a gatehouse staffed by a real person in a uniform. Although I couldn't see below the windows, I was sure the guards had pistols. They'd need guns to protect such a paradise. God placed angels with flaming swords at the gates of Eden, and he placed Leonard at the entrance to Leisure World, a man admittedly overweight but undeniably serious about his work.

What a place! Each house was slightly different from its neighbors, a different shade of peach, a different-postured *saguaro* cactus sprouting from a tidy gravel yard. American flags were everywhere, and in many places—hung slightly lower—the flags of Minnesota, Nebraska, North Dakota. There were two eighteen-hole golf courses that seemed as if they had been poured into the cracks between the houses (I saw people step out of their patios on hole six and simply start golfing), and swarming over the perfect green lanes and ovals of sand were bronzed old people in big sunglasses and floppy hats, all of whom cooed at me as if I were the best little man they had ever seen.

Thirteen-year-old me tied an arrowhead around his neck with a piece of leather string and posed for the camera by Marv and Mil's giant cactus, trying to mimic its awkward stance. By the time I finally made it back to Nashville, I felt like I had visited the most perfect, God-blessed place on Earth. I was sure I wanted to retire there, too.

Of course things changed. I got all Christian-revolutionary and condemned retirement and my grandparents' American made, gas-guzzling Oldsmobile, and then settled into an adult

154

life slightly less radical than I had first envisioned for myself. While I still agreed with most of my nineteen-year-old rants, I went the safer route and stayed behind the scenes through college, writing about all that frontline social justice stuff in articles for a smattering of progressive magazines.

And if anything, I loved Marv and Mil even more, in an adult way, understanding a little more fully the eccentricities of their strange drumming son with an Afro, and all the crazy things in life that might make two people with atrophying bones and ebbing eyesight want to live behind a tall and very strong wall. The world had me reeling a bit, too.

No, they were not weaklings. They had seen much, survived much. My grandparents were "troopers," to borrow some of their own vernacular. They were the "real deal," to use a little of my own.

...

Around 2,286 miles after my wife and I left our home in North Carolina in pursuit of the world's best tree climber, we arrived in Mesa, where we saw Marv and Mil at the door, so glad to see us, offering to help with our bags despite the hundred and ten-degree heat and their collective hundred and eighty-six years of living.

"No Grandpa, we've got it. Thanks!"

And as we threw the bags into our room, Grandma had already gone to get a few photo albums and Grandpa had turned down the golf tournament on TV. We talked for a while, tried to explain Kathryn's graduate research on HIV/AIDS in a city considered ground zero for sex tourism, but the mention of ground zero got them talking about September 11th and the importance of supporting our troops, who had taken the War on Terror to them (the terrorists) instead of them bringing it to us (the inhabitants of Leisure World).

No matter. My wife and I wanted to connect. We had talked

about it since we had decided to detour to Mesa, how few years we had left with Marv and Mil, how important each moment truly was. Kathryn brought Grandpa a recent article of mine, written about a community development group in Atlanta working toward "gentrification with justice" in decaying urban neighborhoods, and he stopped after the first page, looked at her helplessly and said, "Honey, I don't know what this is about."

I didn't know where to begin.

It's just that there are these crazy people who have peeked under the shiny chrome hood of the American dream, Grandpa, and seen a rotting engine grinding up men, women, and children in its pistons—they're the real mechanics, rolling up their sleeves and tinkering with the machine.

No, weird metaphor. Didn't think he'd get it.

It's just that there are these people rejecting affluence and, at times, even safety in order to "neighbor" (read: verb) with the poor, addicted, homeless, and lonely. It's kind of crazy, Grandpa. It's like the Leisure World antitheses. These people are fearless!

But I didn't even begin. He was tracing his finger down the glossy page and furrowing his brow. He was concentrating, straining, but it was too much. He set the magazine down, placed his reading glasses over the page and said, "Thanks for showing me this, honey. It's very interesting."

What was even *more* interesting to Grandpa was *Cops,* as in the TV show, as in every night he tuned in to see the men and women of law enforcement ridding the streets of criminals and "illegals," as Grandma said, referring to undocumented Hispanic workers, the same ones she saw hanging out at a street corner close to Leisure World looking for work.

After *Cops* there was *America's Most Wanted,* and sometimes they stayed up late enough to catch a docudrama about serial killers, drug dealers who murdered their families, or some rightwing news pundits who told Marv and Mil, night after night, that there was a socialist cadre of gay, ambiguously-foreign-or-maybe-Mexican, abortion-loving terrorists who hated all Americans plus Lutherans and who were coming, right then, at the gates or maybe even the door, wanting nothing more than to ruin Social Security, Medicare, old-fashioned goodness and freedom in general.

Marv and Mil trusted Leonard and his pistol at the gate, but they knew he was only one man. They were terrified.

. . .

Great Grandpa Harry, had he survived the pulley, wouldn't have understood Leisure World or Marv and Mil's life within its walls. When he died in 1929, the Social Security act that paved the way for such compounds was still six years away. Although a few retirement communities were popping up in Florida, populated only by wealthy industrialists, the concept of retirement as Marv and Mil had managed it would have seemed as foreign to Harry as communism or late-sixties free love or gentrification married to justice.

Retirement was, in fact, a relatively new phenomenon. Back in the day, or rather *way* back in the day (think Neanderthal), "Any early man who lived long enough to develop crow's-feet was either worshiped or eaten as a sign of respect," writes Mary-Lou Weisman for the *New York Times*. Fast forward to the biblical days of Abraham and, according to Weisman, "When a patriarch could no longer farm, herd cattle or pitch a tent, he opted for more specialized, less labor-intensive work, like prophesying and handing down commandments. Or he moved in with his kids."

Marv and Mil didn't really have that option. Uncle Gary started a perpetually-struggling T-shirt print business, and their youngest, Terry, quickly put down his drumsticks when us kids got hungry and the Love Bucket ran dry. He picked up his paintbrushes and airless sprayers and drop cloths, then proceeded to not make much money painting houses for almost four decades.

No, Grandma and Grandpa would have to fend for themselves. As much as they might have wanted to model their lives on Abrahamic precedent, shacking up with the kids was never a real option. Nor was prophesying.

. . .

Grandma left us in the living room with Grandpa and the news anchors and drifted off to the kitchen where she was preparing a meal. She spent half an hour shuffling around, clanking silverware and mixing things in a bowl, and then pulled a large casserole from the oven.

We gathered. Grandpa sipped on his wine, a "Chillable Red" from a box in the refrigerator, and my wife and I gobbled up Grandma's baked seafood medley covered in Corn Flakes. It was the strangest best thing I'd ever had.

"So you two are traveling a bit?" said Grandpa.

"Sure are," I said. "We're still hoping to find the world's best tree climber, but regardless, we're going to camp our way up the Pacific coast before Kathryn has to fly to Thailand."

There was a pause at the table.

"Do you think that's safe?" asked Grandma. "There are lots of crazies out there."

She might have been referring to the psychotic murderous heathens who had been clawing at her television screen for the last four hours trying to get into her living room.

"We're always safe, Grandma," I said.

But there was a sermon brewing in my belly. It was anti-TV and pro-adventure and antagonistic towards bad punditry. My wife could sense it, this didactic energy growing inside me, the same lecture she had stomached a million times during long car rides, all about fear and the media and how to live ferociously.

She put her hand on mine and said, "We only camp in designated parks where there are rangers."

It was as if Kathryn had just turned a valve, allowing the thickening air around the table to hiss out under the door. Marv and Mil collectively sighed. To them, a good man in a uniform, perhaps even with a firearm, was one of the most beautiful things in the world.

"That's great, honey," said Grandpa. "You can never be too careful."

. . .

It is unlikely that human beings were ever meant to live in Mesa, Arizona. It is a harsh place, with temperatures soaring above a hundred degrees for much of the year, a place full of poisonous things living under rocks and spiky plant life. It is unbelievably dry. So dry that its original inhabitants, the *Hohokam* Nation, had to dig a series of canals through the desert in order to live, to grow edible things, to stay hydrated.

Once the canals were dug, though, Mesa became something of a destination. Spanish missionaries eventually came through proselytizing and converting, and then Daniel Webster Jones and the Mormons decided the area would make a nice place free of angry mobs to dig in their heels. By the turn of the century, Mesa was a bustling little town, and when air-conditioning went mainstream in the late forties, the place exploded.

But there has always been this mystique about the valley, something that draws people looking for havens, for an alternative, for a place to disappear. It worked for the ancient *Hohokam* until the Spanish found them and pounced. It worked for the polygamists of the Church of Latter Day Saints until economic interests diversified the land outside their compounds. And it had worked more recently for the hordes of snowbirds, old folks descending from the Midwest looking for warmth, card games, and protective walls.

And yet the infiltration continued. The "illegals" down the street were just the beginning, according to my grandparents' trusted news sources. There were also the Muslims, the liberals, all those who, unlike my grandfather, failed to ceremonially raise the American flag on a daily basis with patriotic respect.

Much like their grandson. I was, in fact, the progressive enemy at the gates. Worse than that, I was the green-leaning democratic socialist who sailed *past* the gates by flashing a big smile at Leonard and who was, even now, quite happily, settled at the kitchen table eating the seafood medley. Marv and Mil had no idea.

...

My dad, after his divorce from Mom, asked Mil if he could move out to Leisure World to take care of her and Grandpa. Mil politely said no way.

To be fair, there were certain rules that clearly stated no family members of homeowners were allowed to stay for longer than a month. This was to ensure that the pesky relatives of retirees didn't clog up the pool or exercise room or woodshop. It happened. Things got busy around there in winter, and the old folks liked to have plenty of space for their in-pool volleyball games and horseshoes.

Dad was a little disappointed. He had been painting houses since he was in his late-twenties and much of his parents' life out in Mesa was, quite simply, fantastical. Like a gingerbread house. Pinocchio's carnival. The Big Rock Candy Mountain where one could sleep all day because the authorities "hung the jerk who invented work."

There were also the Muslims. Dad was suspicious of them. The Muslims had an "agenda" according to the books he read and the right-wing radio hosts he listened to. *Sharia* law was poised to eclipse the Constitution as soon as he let his guard down, so he remained vigilant. I'm not sure when it happened, but his evangelical faith was fused with a kind of patriotic paranoia, and the twelve-foot walls of Leisure World—surrounding a predominantly white Christian population from the Midwest—had become particularly enticing.

Dad was the exact age as Grandpa when he retired with a

modest but sufficient pension, plus a modest but sufficient social security check. Dad, with his fishy taxes over the years, was less than confident the government would similarly take care of him. Instead of retiring, he was still dragging buckets of paint up tall ladders in mid-day heat, living paycheck to paycheck, eating food out of cans and scraping together money for rent (to say nothing of retirement), and all with a lower back that still threatened, daily, to give up once and for all.

He went to visit his folks every few years, sleep late, walk outside to pick grapefruit for breakfast before smacking golf balls into holes all day. No work. No Muslims. He would have moved in an instant.

"Thanks but no thanks," said Mil, who insisted she didn't need anyone to care for her in old age. "We get along out here just fine."

She had, after all, dominated the Leisure World Women's Senior Golf Tournament for decades, and had only recently slowed down on the course. And Grandpa, as I found out that morning, was still active enough to daily hit the gym, pressing and curling and squatting. We stopped by the nurses' office on the way home to check his blood pressure. A little high, that day, but not to worry.

"It's up and down all the time," he said. "It's probably just because we've been so excited to see you kids."

...

After dinner we all wandered back to the living room to digest a little before going to bed. Kathryn and I would be gone in the morning, back on the road for points west. The television continued to saturate the room with senseless murder and pollution reports, and Marv and Mil continued to feel more and more grateful for their little sanctuary, their square mile of peace.

"Now they've got a recall on beef," said Grandpa, speaking generically to the room in his gravely baritone. "Man-o-man. I don't know why they can't discover it before they ship it. That's what gets me."

What got *me* was that I wasn't sure I would see Marv and Mil again. There were always a few years between visits, and Kathryn and I, mired as we were in new marriage, graduate school, and life in general, would probably not get back to Mesa for a long time. And time, as it related to Marv and Mil, was a precious, precarious commodity.

The next morning I hugged my grandparents with all my might, as deeply as I could without hurting their frail bones and, before pointing the little Honda westward with Bernd Strasser on my mind, I did my best to stamp their wrinkled, smiling faces into my memory. I wanted crisp edges. Here stood Marv and Mil Andersen, arm in arm, alive, healthy and safe. They had settled here all the way from Sioux City, having survived wave after troubled wave of life, and now there was a cactus behind them, a crow overhead, and all around a desert subdued by sprinkler systems and exotic landscaping. They had been faithful, hardworking, and their lives—despite the high blood pressure and undocumented workers down the street—were plugging along just fine behind the walls.

. . .

Kathryn and I took our car to get the tires aligned and the air conditioning serviced. The opressive desert heat was taxing the system to its limit. As we waited for the Civic to reemerge I got a text from Mom saying that she and Danielle had just left Sam Donald's farm, finally releasing their hold on the old acres. Danielle was nineteen years old, my adopted baby sister who wasn't so much a baby anymore, who had never seen big mountains except on television, who had been in something of a downward spiral ever since Mom and Dad split up. Danielle wasn't doing well, Mom texted. She suggested I call. And then it struck me: Danielle could fly into Seattle as my wife flew out, and together we could meander all over the West until we had seen everything there was to see. "It would be pivotal for her," I told my wife. "A new beginning! A hinge moment! A trip across the country with me at the helm might be just the jumpstart she's been needing to get her life in motion again!"

My wife quickly punched holes in my hubris. She had become adept at exactly that: puncturing the balloon of my messiah complex, which tended to inflate often. But I still decided to reach out. And it was an easy enough sell: "Hey, Danielle, why don't you fly out west so we can drive back east together."

"Really?"

"Yeah, it will be, um, pivotal."

"Sure!" she said, without asking what I meant.

Indeed, we flex. Bernd Strasser, the best tree climber in the world, stepped deeper into the shadows of his sequoias where I imagined him coiling his ropes in peace. My grandparents diminished in our rear view mirror as we hurtled toward the Pacific on Interstate 10. My baby sister, Danielle, whose suicide attempts over the last few years had been frequent, who had been institutionalized for the omnipresent depression and anxiety, who, at nineteen, had yet to see a real mountain, stepped quietly into the light.

...

Danielle was the youngest of six girls. She left the maternity ward after a few days, spent a week in an old crumbling house in north Nashville, and was then snatched from her mother's arms by a state caseworker on the front steps. The official narrative was that each of her sisters had been abused in some way, and her mother, who had been in and out of jail, was essentially state-ordered not to produce more progeny lest they be swept away.

We were a fresh new foster family. It was Mom who pushed for the role, convincing Dad that my brother, sister, and I were getting older, self-sufficient, and that it was time to foster or adopt some kids in need. It was the Christian thing to do. Dad, of course, was endlessly painting houses and was more reluctant than Mom to start over. My siblings and I had already demanded so much, taken so much, filled our parents' lives with all kinds of adolescent angst, drugs, and sleepless nights. But Mom was insistent, and the paperwork went through, and suddenly we got a call one night to ask if we'd foster a week-old baby girl who had just been whisked away from a purportedly fiendish family.

This is what I remember: the humidity and the honeysuckle. Our condominium complex before we found Sam Donald's farm and all the blacktop and me tearing over the blacktop on my skateboard, soaring over drainage ditches and patches of grass and bright yellow speed bumps. I remember shooting up the steps of our deck and sliding open the heavy glass door and then there was a baby in Mom's arms, a quiet little human being all wrapped in pink, and I remember my dad calling for my brother and sister upstairs, calling them down to the dining room where the baby slept in Mom's arms. He told us to lay our hands on her and pray for her, told us that God had spared her all kinds of abuse and torture and brought her to us, which was a kind of salvation. I had stopped believing in God in those days but I closed my eyes as tightly as I could, laid my hand on the baby, and asked God to forgive my unbelief long enough to hear my prayer, which was that the baby would be safe and healthy and that she would never have to go back to her birth family again. I opened my eyes, shoved my hands back in my pockets, and silently said *amen*.

. . .

Danielle and I made a pact. Well, actually *I* created a pact for our trip that she essentially agreed to. I told her she was free to add her own ideas, but mine seemed to take up a lot of space. Not much room for additions.

This is what I said:

- You: No high fructose corn syrup drinks (Dr. Pepper).
- Me: No alcohol.
- Us: Daily exercise, journal entries, healthy eating.
- You: No going home.
- Me: I will share control of the music.
- Us: We will be honest if annoyed, communicate openly and freely.
- You: NO BOYS!

Mom said Danielle had printed out the pact and hung it on her wall, right next to all the pictures of ex-boyfriends who had been less than loving towards her. She agreed to our pre-trip training program, which included exercise and lots of drinking water. She started to search for tickets and tried to fight back the growing anxiety attached to getting on a plane for the first time by herself.

And I gave up on my strength training for the Strasser interview and simply worked my way slowly up the coast with my wife, wondering the whole time if Danielle would actually get on the plane. The last time she had tried to fly was on a visit to my college in Philadelphia, with the understanding that she might even stay with us for a while. She had made it all the way to the ticket counter, bought the one-way ticket, and then went fetal on the airport floor. Mom phoned from the terminal and called the whole thing off.

Danielle said over the phone that it wouldn't happen again, that she would definitely come, but later Mom said that my sister had been having "swings" and "melt downs." The day before she was scheduled to fly, Danielle tried to hurt herself again, this time with sleeping pills. She was back from the hospital and okay, but Mom thought she did it because she failed to exercise enough, felt like she had broken the pact already, and was afraid of what I'd say.

I thought of my baby sister with a tube down her throat, her stomach pumped. I thought of her getting to the airport only to turn around again. I was lost in my own dreams enough to think that if she could just make it, the mountains—and me as guide—would be all she'd really need.

...

As my wife and I moved up the coast, aiming for Seattle, I couldn't stop thinking about two things: my grandparents and their fear, and the young woman I was about to meet and spend the next two weeks travelling with. In those moments of winding highway when I was most honest with myself, I recognized the deep, suffocating fear in me, too. In some ways I had been trying to fight it back forever.

One of my first memories was hearing my parents arguing downstairs, late at night with a quiet urgency in the old house in Freeville. They were hissing at each other through their teeth.

I snuck over to the stairs, only three, maybe four years old, and I remember hearing an accusation, a defense, the mention of another woman's name. A kind of electricity came over me and I was paralyzed with fear.

I was afraid to fly. To cross tall bridges. I was afraid I wouldn't do anything of consequence with my short life. I was afraid, after studying that semester's worth of astronomy in undergrad, that our planet was far more precarious than most of us cared to admit. That we were, in fact, sitting ducks for anything the universe might throw at us, including our own life-giving sun as soon as it decided to eat itself once and for all.

And for some reason my fears seemed to grow as my wife and I drove further up the coast, her eyes set on Thailand, me thinking almost exclusively of my grandparents behind and my sister ahead. A night of camping by the ocean found me not lulled off to sleep by the waves, but instead wide awake as I imagined a tsunami sweeping us away in the night. I actually felt the ground tremble and, before realizing it was a distant RV's generator, I was paralyzed just like I had been at the top of the stairs.

It was getting thick, this fear. It felt like it was shooting through everything. As we pulled up to Seattle's airport, I couldn't stop thinking about what it would be like to never see my wife again. I kissed her goodbye, watched her disappear behind the opaque security glass. I waited until she was far into the terminal and only then began accepting the fact that she would spend the next month researching her way through the red light districts of Bangkok and that I, at the rate I was going, might somehow finally wreck my sister's life by trying to save it.

I had received a text earlier that day, Mom telling me that Danielle was on the plane after only a few tears. I got another text, this time from Danielle. She said she was on her way. My texting thumbs came to life and I reminded her that this plane ride, which was really just a mouse of an issue, had become a monster for her. I told her to slay the monster. "Kick the monster's ass," I said. "You are a soldier, a champion. You're Joan of Arc."

Another botched metaphor. Her phone clicked to sleep and I imagined the plane doors suctioning shut and the pressurized air filling the cabin. I imagined her gripping the inoperable ashtrays, closing her sore eyes and cringing as the jet engines roared to life like lions.

. . .

When Danielle was eight years old, she told me she hated me, so I locked her in a closet. By this time we were living in Sam Donald's old house. The closet was one of his many renovations. I don't remember why Danielle told me she hated me, but after the outburst I can remember feeling that I was the one to finally set her straight, get her on the right track. The idea of the closet came quickly. I grabbed her by the arm and marched her into her own room, into her own closet, pulled the light on and slammed the door shut.

167

I, too, was on the inside. I figured if I locked her in there alone she might just sit and fume and devise all kinds of terrible revenges against me. So I stayed with her. I sat there as she clawed for the door handle, but I kept her at bay with one arm and picked up Veggie Tales tapes with the other, started reading all of the backs of the VHS boxes out loud. Very loud:

Have you ever felt too small to do a really big job? That's what a little shepherd boy named Dave feels when his big brothers head off to defend their country, leaving him behind with the sheep. They're in for a surprise when they find out their foe is a 9-foot pickle!

Probably the worst parenting move ever. I, of course, wasn't even a parent. I just made it up, as it was the only thing that came to mind in the moment. Strangely enough it seemed to work. We stayed in there until she calmed down and started talking. We agreed that she couldn't say hateful things to me or anyone else anymore, and I finally set her free, sort of apologized for locking her away, but also made a mental note to file the technique away in case my as-yet-unborn kids got born and started acting unruly.

The truth was I had always tried to fix people. Siblings, parents, politicians—the whole world. I screamed at the nightly news sometimes fully believing that if the people on the screen would actually listen to me, the planet might finally find its equilibrium. I suffered from this severe middle-kid psychosis-plus-self-delusion that encouraged me to believe I could make everyone feel happy and healthy all the time, if only I worked hard enough.

Danielle had been on my fix-it list for a long time. I noted the changes in her, the growing mood swings and depression as my parents' marriage began to crumble. She was only fourteen when it started, still planted firmly at the farm without an escape hatch. I tried at times to stretch myself from my relatively stable adult life into her darkening adolescent one and pluck her out. I reached and reached but eventually saw her slip beneath all the tumult—the little girl Danielle seemed to drift away, and the girl who floated back to the surface was someone different indeed. This new Danielle went into her room, slammed the door shut, and began taking sharp objects to her skin, channeling every bit of fear and anger and lack of control into the press of a pen tip against her flesh.

. . .

The Seattle airport in summer was bright and huge and clean. It felt fresh and hopeful. After my wife disappeared through the security gate I watched the arrivals intently, saw all the explosions of happiness and gratitude—people together again, finally. But even the departures had this sweetness and sadness all mixed together. A group of ten teenagers stood to my right, saying goodbye to a girl, Yuki, who was heading back to her home in Japan. Ten teenagers wept and laughed as they circled her, touching her shoulders and wrapping their arms around her, hungry for simple touch, any connection, before she flew away.

My baby sister walked through the security gate staring at her feet. She was straight-faced, walking slowly, nothing but a book bag and a sweatshirt and the rainbow-laced hiking shoes I asked her to bring so we could walk in the woods.

"You can't fix her," my wife said before leaving. "You can't even fix yourself. All you can do is love her."

"Sure," I said, even as I concocted plans to both love *and* fix her, myself, my grandparents and everything everywhere.

I yelled Danielle's name and her head jerked up as if she had been sleepwalking. Now she was in my arms, breathless from the walking, and I began demanding all the details of her flight and her thoughts, all the things she felt as the plane took off, leveled out, landed.

She was good. Sedated with anxiety medicine, tired and

hungry. But good. Now it was me and Danielle and an entire country lying to our right—the East. We walked slowly to the car, paid our parking ticket at a little kiosk, and threw her bag on top of the pile of books and clothes and camping gear scattered around the Civic. Evidence of a proper road trip.

"You ready?" I asked.

"I'm ready," she said.

"Do you like fish and chips?"

She made a face like she had just swallowed a cut lemon.

"Well, then I'm going to take you to get the best macaroni and cheese you've ever had," I said, throwing the car in gear, heading straight for Pike Place Market, feeling grateful for the heat and light of the Northwestern sun, grateful that all the rumors of rain, at least for that day, were verifiably untrue.

...

Danielle had been writing for a long time, ever since she was a little girl. She never read much, at least not until the *Lord of the Rings* trilogy seduced her into Middle Earth, but she was always creative and found it easy to put good stories together.

I had been handing out writing assignments for a long time, to just about anyone who would politely accept them. Danielle was always a prime candidate because she never turned them down and always delivered startling, fresh stories written with a genuine and steady prose.

So as we drove away from Seattle and pulled the car onto a ferry at Whidbey Island, I was lost in narratives, thinking about the storylines that captivate us and all the ways we try to live out those storylines in our real lives. For me, the narratives that had dominated my life were the ones in which heroes (usually having started out as pig keepers or mild-mannered something-or-others) discover their true calling and go on to save the universe. Yes, that's my story, I thought and felt and believed every time I saw it in a film or read it in a book. The hero's journey to defeat the dragon and return with the elixir. I then tended to inflict my narrative on all those around me, like a comic book hero who swoops down to rescue pedestrians on their way to work, spilling coffee and stepping on toes as he "saves" the day.

By the time we pulled off the ferry at Whidbey Island, I decided I had Danielle's narrative figured out, too. It always involved a broken, helpless girl who met a mysterious boy and was then swept up, saved, made whole by his love. It helped if there was something supernatural, lots of lingering looks, occasional vampire teeth.

This was the story she projected onto every goober of a guy she shared a passing smile with, the story she believed and desired above all stories, the one that frequently wiggled its way into her own writing and the one she dreamt about when her dreams were strong enough to break through the medication.

"I've met a boy online," she said as we began driving again. "He's nice."

"Oh," I said. "Tell me about him."

"Not much to say. Lives in Arizona. Works at a grocery store."

I felt desperate to have the narrative conversation with her as we wound our way up Whidbey, but instead I spent the time pointing out all the things she wouldn't have ever seen back home. The sea and boats, the conifer forests and mountainous backdrop and all the shades of prickly green.

I reminded myself of my wife's words even as my messiah narrative bubbled up in me like a rank geyser. You're just here to listen, support, encourage, I told myself as we set up the tent and went for a walk around Deception Pass. You can't save her, I told myself as she wheezed next to me, exhausted from the hundred-yard walk to the waterside. My narrative interrupted, *hrumphed*, and said if I didn't save her, who else possibly could?

. . .

I should have never become a tree climber. If it hadn't have been for my brother's patience I would have stayed forever on the ground, shoving brush into a chipper, raking up the refuse. I still feel the stomach-quivering old fear every time I pass over a tall bridge, get close to any edge with a corresponding drop off. The fear starts in my belly and then overtakes my brain, turns all my thoughts into flashing red DANGER.

Bernd Strasser didn't feel the same fear. Nor did my big brother, who instead had spent his entire life looking for the next perilous edge.

Danielle, of course, had a list of fears as long as a complex curry recipe. All kinds of social anxieties, fear of dogs, fear of being alone.

And yet a few months before our trip she dove from a plane at fourteen thousand feet strapped to a stranger named Junior. My brother was there because that's where he was most weekends, still doing his best to feel alive by taunting death.

Danielle was just supposed to go down to the drop zone and hang out, read a book or two and take some pictures. But my brother had this funny up-and-at-em influence, this way of talking people into doing things they wouldn't normally do: one more shot of tequila or a pedal-to-the-metal race or a free fall from a plane. He worked on Danielle for a few hours and then, suddenly, before she knew what was really happening, she was suited up, given instructions, and hoisted into the air by an old prop plane piloted by a chain-smoking hippie with a ponytail.

She jumped, face first, falling directly into Aaron who had grabbed her by the shoulder straps and pulled her into himself, him plummeting at a hundred miles an hour on his back and laughing like crazy as Danielle and Junior chased him through the sky. He had a video camera attached to his helmet and I had seen the footage, her face all contorted by the wind, the fear turning into something like high-voltage joy as she realized, half way to the earth, that she was momentarily flying.

When she got safely to the ground, she called to tell me

what she had done.

"Guess what?"

"What?"

"I jumped!"

"Out of a plane? Seriously?"

"Seriously! I'll send you pictures!"

And then a grainy shot of Danielle in a jumpsuit materialized on my cell phone, she and Aaron giving the lens some kind of *hell yeah* gesture, tongues out, arms draped over shoulders.

I was amazed and simultaneously jealous that my brother was the one to unlock such an adventure in Danielle. I usually felt like I was the only one capable of such things. That it was somehow my job.

But mostly I was just amazed. And along with a list of other things, I had been meaning to make my baby sister a little laminated card that she could keep in her purse, a card that she could pull out every time a panic attack came in a throng of people, or when anxiety over an upcoming driver's test or GED exam built to a breaking point:

> I, Danielle, jumped from an airplane at fourteen thousand feet, flew through the air, and landed upright on my feet. I, Danielle, can do anything, survive anything, conquer any fear.

I planned to include a little thumbnail picture of her in her purple jumpsuit—a proof, a stake in the ground, a talisman that she could hold up like a lamp against any darkness.

. . .

We drove north through the Cascade mountain range, endless curves, perfect view after perfect view. We dropped down through a reservation and stopped at Coulee Dam. I couldn't help myself and started getting didactic, lecturing my sister about the rounding up and sequestering of Native Americans. I ranted about electricity, as in what happens when we flip on light switches in our homes, all about the destructive nature of coal plants and dams and reactors.

She simply wanted air conditioning. It was hot in the wheat fields of eastern Washington. I turned it on reluctantly, mumbling about decreased gas mileage, and watched her watching her hand trace the curvature of the fields. She realized that if she squinted with one eye and pumped her fingers along the landscape as it whizzed by, it looked like her fingers were running up and down the passing green hills. She pulled out her camera, switched it to video, and recorded her fingers tippy-toeing along at seventy miles an hour.

There was laughter now, hers and mine. She showed me the video and indeed it looked like her hand was running a breakneck marathon over the hills. Looked like even her hand was flying.

"It's beautiful out here," she said.

Soon we were out of gas. Danielle had never filled up a tank. Pumping gas had always been Mom's job and Mom never asked her to help. I showed her how it was done, how to slide the card in and swipe it quickly, how not to fill an unleaded tank with diesel. She was open to these lessons and didn't grumble. I scrubbed away the insect carcasses from the windshield and she replaced the pump and it all felt like something of a victory.

And although the goal was to drink only water and juice on the trip, she wandered through the gas station and saw a sport drink with the triumvirate lure of being "cheap, big, and cold." She bought it under the auspices of hydration and brought it to the car, reading through the ingredients as she settled into her seat.

There was water in that bottle, high fructose corn syrup, a smattering of electrolytes and vitamins and unpronounceable chemicals.

"I broke the pact," she sighed. "I didn't know."

She handed me the bottle and I turned it over in my hands, studied the label and swirled the bright blue liquid into a funnel.

"It seemed like the kind of thing that wouldn't have syrup in it," she said apologetically. "I'm sorry."

My heart sank because I had been the one to put all these pressures on Danielle. I had tried so hard to simply let the trip flow, be what it would be, but I couldn't stop trying to throw some scaffolding at it. I was so desperate to create a pivot point in her life, a fulcrum that would allow her to teeter away from all these destructive habits and patterns. More water, less lethargy, daily doses of hope. It was a heavy load for a quick trip across the country. And I was failing to keep her from the weight of my own expectations.

"No worries, kid. Stupid labels. Small print. Now you know."

We moved on, blasting east, her sipping at the sports drink and me pounding out familiar paradiddles onto the steering wheel: *right-left-left, left-right-right*. We hit the interstate and cruised at eighty. We had never really spent much time together and somewhere in the middle of Montana she said, "Okay, let's get to know each other," and she told me all about the boys she had loved and how they had hurt her. She described what it was like to be stuck at home as Mom and Dad's marriage dismantled. We collectively remember the closet and the Veggie Tale tapes.

"I'm glad you still don't hate me," I said. "I guess the closet worked."

"Yeah right," she said with a smirk. "I just wanted to get out of there."

I dreamed of a bottomless gas tank and the ability to show Danielle everything. But everything didn't exist on a single road headed east. Everything was everywhere—Glacier to our north, the Dakota Badlands straight east. I was putting out feelers to see if the impossibly large faces of former presidents carved into a mountain was something she'd like to see. Or maybe Canada, a first visit for her to a foreign country. What did she want? What did she need? I studied the map as if it were a sacred text,

tracing my finger along highways connected to interstates connected to little swathes of green (National Parks) and brown
(reservations) and realized I was looking everywhere for real-
time answers.

"How about Yellowstone?" I asked.

"What's there?"

"All kinds of stuff. Bears, moose, geysers. Old Faithful!"

"Old Faithful!"

"Only the most famous geyser in the world. We have to
see it!"

And this was how we made our decisions. We headed south
to Yellowstone to see water erupting faithfully from the earth. I
brought my map as we sat in the shade of a tree, waiting for the
aquatic fireworks, and I calculated distances and mouthed the
names of towns.

"Kit Carson, Colorado," I mumbled. "I wonder what it's
like down there."

Steam was hissing from a hole in a ground and a few hundred people lounged in a giant circle, playing with the buttons
on their electronic equipment. Old Faithful seemed to be teasing
us, sending up plumes of steam and then subsiding. We heard
people say *This is it* and *It's coming now,* but still we waited.

I took our bottles into the cafeteria to pilfer fresh water
from the soda fountain and when I came back the geyser was
more active.

"Are you ready for it?" I asked, noticing too late that Danielle's eyes were rimmed in red and wet with tears.

"Sure," she said, wiping at her face with the back of her
hand.

"You okay?"

"Sure," she said, pointing her camera at the geyser as it
erupted, spraying us and hundreds of others with a mineral-rich
mist. Her crying disappeared in the wet air.

"Okay, let's boogie so we beat traffic," I said, and we shuffled back to the car to find a campsite before dark.

Her heart broke a hundred times a day, it seemed. Sometimes it healed for a while—she would smile and laugh—and then the cracks would open up all over again. I had no idea what to do. I had hoped the landscape itself might work like a tonic, and I, the humble chaperone, could simply introduce her to it.

As Yellowstone vanished quickly in our rearview mirror, I began writing her a letter in my mind. It started like this:

Dear Danielle,

I don't want you to die.

And it went on to describe all the things I wished she might experience in life, the sensations that might make it feel worth living, the multitude of ways she might get healthy and avoid onset diabetes by the time she was thirty, regain control of her emotions and relationships. But these letters, in many ways, were exactly the problem. This had been my wife's warning.

We rode together without saying much, eventually finding a little camping spot on a ridge where we could see the entire Teton mountain range. It was getting dark, dark enough that the stars were beginning to materialize in the sky above us. Our friend told us that we could see more stars out there than anywhere else in the country.

After the tent I set up our little camp chairs and positioned them facing the mountains and sat down to wait for the light show. Danielle said she was going to sleep.

"But the stars," I said.

"I'm just really tired," she said, and she zipped up the tent and began to flirt over text with a stranger in Arizona.

I took my chair further into the darkness and watched the sky. Satellites patrolled space, tiny pinpricks of light soaring slowly above. And there were shooting stars, which of course are just bits of space dust burning up in our atmosphere. Every thirty seconds or so I saw another sail past. Before long I heard the whining of wolves, and then the howls. I thought of the coyotes back home, the ridge of Sam Donald's farm. Danielle had given up texting and was talking now, sending kisses into the receiver and telling the boy, "I love you."

Finally the phone clicked shut and there was silence. I waited for a long time out in the darkness and when I heard her gentle snoring I sighed and realized I had been clenching my teeth, as if waiting for a punch to land. I realized I had carried the anxiety of the day in my shoulders since morning. I let them sag, slouched deep into the chair and prayed for the first time in a long time, again asking God to listen past my unbelief and save my sister. Especially from her own brother.

. . .

Bernd Strasser never showed up for that year's tree climbing championship. I'm not sure if the Sequoias wore him out, or if he just felt like it was time to move on. The new champion was a climber named Jared Abrojena from the Western chapter. He was clean-shaven, with short-cropped hair and a smiling, all-American face. I could see him on the cover of *GQ* or *Outside*, but I was still banking on Strasser. Eight out of the last ten championships was still pretty good. I sent another email from Fort Collins, Colorado, assuring him there were no hard feelings, that if he'd like I could meet him anywhere in the world with my ropes and recorder. I'm still waiting for him to respond.

Danielle and I continued to drive East through some of the most magnificent landscape on the planet in perfect summer sunshine, yet I couldn't seem to shake a feeling of imminent doom that started north of Mesa. Yes, the music was just right. The windows mostly down. But I kept thinking about my parents and Sam Donald's farm and my brother's increasingly dangerous dives and the little sister sitting in the seat next to mine, riding mostly in silence. I thought of the sex tourists passing my wife on the sidewalks of Thailand, some with two or three pre-pubescent girls hanging on their arms. I kept thinking of the televangelists from my parents TV, the ones my dad used to watch late at night when he wasn't sleeping with his wife in the room next door, the spiritual schemers who were now targeting inner-city African Americans and retirees, having sucked dry the rural white Midwest in the 80s and 90s. I thought of my grandparents and their delicate bodies and all the ways in which they had tried to insulate themselves. And I thought of the impersonal cruelty of our cosmos and asteroids and the destruction of dinosaurs, perhaps a harbinger of what's on its way for us. No matter where Danielle and I drove, we always seemed to look into the sky and see a palpable haze of pollution hanging in the horizon like a grainy television screen long past its scheduled programming. Somewhere in the middle of Oklahoma everything just went gray.

After Danielle and I got back to Tennessee I dropped her off at Mom's new place, hugged her deeply, and immediately drove to my brother's house, where I waited for my wife to return from Thailand. I threw my stuff on Aaron's couch and grabbed his remote control, hit the big green button, and tried to disappear into the programming.

"You okay?" he asked late on the first night.

"Just catching up with the world," I said, rubbing bloodshot eyes.

Two days after we arrived home from our three-thousand-mile trip, Mom called to tell me Danielle had taken twenty-eight pills and was whisked away to the hospital by three police cars, two ambulances, and one fire truck. Mom said the lights around the rental house filled the neighborhood as if it were the Fourth of July.

Danielle was quickly stabilized, and by the time I was able to see her in the hospital she was already taking a kind of after-care class and doing better. We talked on the phone, too, and sometimes I would send her a text, reminding her to go outside and get some vitamin D, or to drink more water so she could keep hydrated.

"Thanks," she'd say. "Thanks for the reminder."

It was a small screen where all those words transferred back and forth, where all those words lived and were stored. I always told her I loved her and, even with a smattering of exclamation points, the phrase fit on a single line.

There were times I wanted to write it big, times I wished my texting thumbs connected to a skywriter, one of those bi-planes trailing smoke, not that dissimilar to the kind Danielle leapt from in order to fly. That way she could see the message, and maybe God, too. If I could I would have screamed it perma-nently into the ether, what I had failed to say, simply, all summer long, and perhaps my entire faith-fractured life: *I'm here, Danielle. I'm right here.*

. . .

I met my wife at her arrival in Atlanta and we settled into the old seats of the Civic. She asked about my time with Danielle. All I could think of was how I planned to make a little card for her, the one with the picture of her soaring through the sky, how I would choose a strong font, put it in bold, laminate it. It's all I had. I told her the morbid math of Danielle's return home.

"I think we're all bankrupt," I said.

"What are you talking about?"

"Us, people, human beings. I think our species is on its way out."

"You've been watching TV again, haven't you."

She was right. She could sense the fact that I had been feed-ing on the television. If she only knew how much, how many hours of *Shark Week*, Fox commentators and televangelists, how many music videos and docudramas about the bands who made the videos. If she only knew that *I* knew the entire sordid story of *Guns n' Roses*.

"There's a reason we keep the TV in the closet," she said. "You can't handle it. It gets into your head. You turn into your grandparents."

My grandparents! A little flash of indignation turned my

face hot. No way. I would never move into a gated community and chaff at the thought of outsiders. My heroes were those wacky people moving into bad neighborhoods to be good neighbors despite the gunshots, despite everything on the evening news.

"No way," I muttered as I mulled over her statement, feeling little pangs that might just be truth. "I'm not scared," I said as we rocketed away from Atlanta through the pollution, through an endless corridor of brightly-lit billboards hocking fried chicken, cell phone service, advanced home security systems promising a little peace of mind.

...

Grandpa Marv said the same thing, the same catch phrase, after every bit of news, good or bad.

"For crying out loud," he said, elated, when we arrived at Leisure World that summer to visit. "For crying out loud," he said again when he heard about the recall on beef, or when a server brought him a large orange juice instead of a small.

I never really understood the phrase, even though I had heard it since I was a kid. It just seemed normal, natural, like the breath one takes before speaking or the exhale after one has finished.

When Kathryn and I arrived back home I tried it out, after reading a particularly disturbing headline about health care. I said it quietly, to myself.

"For crying out loud," I said. "Who the hell brings automatic weapons to a presidential town hall meeting?"

And then, just for a moment, there was a kind of peace.

Alongside my messiah complex, my wife diagnosed me with "mean world syndrome," a term used to describe the paranoia and fear that can occur after one has been inundated by the violence and general bad newsiness of mainstream media. It turns out that after enough *Nightline* and *Cops*, one can start to see the world strictly through those quick edit montages of human evil and natural disasters.

Of course Kathryn and I liked to diagnose each other frequently, mainly to win an argument or prove a point.

This time, though, I think she might have been right. I Googled it, and everything I found on mean world syndrome seemed to match up with not only my experience, but also with the vibe out in my grandparents' living room. It seems that no matter how tall one builds those walls, the outside world still creeps in through little electric plugs and, ironically, becomes even scarier than real life.

For crying out loud.

Things were a little better after my wife and I got home. The TV stayed in the closet and I periodically checked my email to see if Bernd Strasser had gotten back. I texted often with Danielle, who seemed to be stabilized and doing better. I even called my brother and let him describe, over and over again, the sensation of the next level of his skydiving, which was called "swooping," an advanced landing technique that had become its own international sub-competition in which divers plummet from the sky and use their chutes to skim across water or around obstacles placed on the ground, inches above terra firma at eighty miles an hour.

For the rest of that summer I found that many days I surrendered to the nagging sense that if the televangelists didn't ruin everything, the Texas-sized asteroid I saw on that show, the one with the computer animation of Earth getting smashed to bits, was just around the cosmic corner.

Other days I simply meditated on Mil, who was scheduled to turn ninety-five in two weeks. My dad and Uncle Gary were shelving their low-paying jobs and flying out to Mesa to celebrate, but Kathryn and I were stuck on the East coast, having burned up all of our travel money that summer. Instead of an in-the-flesh reunion, Kathryn put a card in the mail that communicated as well as a card could how much we loved Mil, appreciated her, and wanted her to live forever.

These were facts.

And there are more. The asteroid is undoubtedly coming and the televangelists seem to have won this round. An eighteen-year-old Muslim detonates the bomb strapped to her chest and my father, on the other side of the world, at home alone with his tired painter bones, whispers her strange, lilting name with venom.

Someday Grandma will die.

There is already a cancer in Grandpa, eating.

"Expect the end of the world," says the Wendell Berry poem that, like a life raft, had been keeping me afloat those days. And then it says, "Laugh. Laughter is immeasurable. Be joyful though you have considered all the facts."

Because the truth is, the only real antidote for the pervasive sense that this planet is socially, environmentally, politically and infrastructurally imploding is to grab onto something, a sliver of faith, a hearty *for-crying-out-loud*, a poem that encourages you to put your trust in the "two inches of humus that will build under the trees every thousand years."

And then to act.

"Love someone who does not deserve it," writes Berry. Love despite the facts. "Praise ignorance, for what man has not encountered he has not destroyed."

I spoke these things into the air that summer though I wanted to send them directly to Danielle, to my grandparents. I wanted them all to understand. My brother and sisters. Mom and Dad. I wanted them to know that I was scared, too, more than ever before, terrified of all the things that seemed to be swirling around those days, a kind of evil, a dust that settled over everything. Even the horizon.

But I said this to Danielle: "You jumped from a plane and flew through the sky staring into the wild eyes of your brother who loves you."

I quoted this to Grandpa: "Invest in the millennium," Marv.

"Plant sequoias."

I said these things into the air. And then I finally made that card, laminated it, sent it Danielle's way.

"We love you so much and will see you again soon," I wrote.

I made another card for Grandma saying the exact same thing, although I sensed the precariousness of these particular facts.

No matter.

"Practice resurrection," I said as my sister made her way back to her normal life in a new house with Mom.

"Practice resurrection," I said as my father boarded a plane for Leisure World, eyed his fellow passengers suspiciously, and again as the plane touched down in the dust.

"Practice resurrection," I said to my brother as he soared through the air in his flight suit, waiting longer and longer each time to pull his chord before hitting the ground. For the thrill of it. To feel alive.

"Practice resurrection," I said to my wife as she slept in the other room, a book on her chest that rose and fell with her warm breath. We are here and together and alive.

Say that your main crop is the forest
That you did not plant,
That you will not live to harvest.
Say that the leaves are harvested
When they have rotted into the mold.

. . .

I went to her and lay down and closed my eyes.

Eleven

My big brother finally celebrated three decades of life, God bless him. Thirty years of almost-but-never-quite dying.

He should have never lived past eighteen. That was the magic number from the time we were kids, the hinge moment at which he figured he would finally get evened up with all his death defying. The delicate seesaw balance of life was supposed to have long ago tipped—he, of course, had been doing cartwheels and handstands on it all his life—sending him headlong into darkness.

I had been waiting for the fall since I was five and said the Sinner's Prayer. I mean, my brother once stole a tank of refrigerator Freon and huffed it with his head inside a garbage bag to prolong the high. He passed out over and over again. For a week.

But he shot past eighteen unscathed and got his day job, clipping chainsaws to a harness and spiking his way to the tops of long-dead stalks of trees, past mushrooms blossoming from decay, all marshmallow insides, setting up his pulleys and ropes, dismantling giant woody biomasses day after day.

Thirty years, God bless him. That's a long time. He commemorated it with a gin-soaked, hell-of-a-celebration. He wasn't scared of death at all, having seen it so close, almost finger-tip-touched it so many times.

"Let's do something big!" he said. The Eagle Scout, who was with him at the bar, suggested that a good way to squeeze all the juice from the night would be to finally do something about the statue of Nathan Bedford Forrest planted alongside I-65 to greet northbound travelers into Nashville. Bedford Forrest: Confederate general, original Grand Wizard for a freshly formed Ku Klux Klan, a menacing welcome to Music City.

The statue, erected in 1998, was the empirically-proven ugliest thing in the world. Everyone my brother and the Eagle

Scout ever asked said so. Forrest's silver face frozen in a kind of violent hysteria. A golden horse as disgruntled as his rider. A stand of confederate flags swaying in the breeze behind.

Local journalist, David Ribar, once wrote that it was little more than a glorified billboard, a politico-religious screed intended to shout in the face of a commuting audience.

And a whole lot of commuters were successfully pissed off. Nashvillians shot at the statue, cursed it, gave it the finger while screaming by at 80 miles-an-hour.

Yet each morning it still stood.

"Not tonight," said the Eagle Scout. "It'll come down."

My brother's thirtieth was the right time to finally strike—something big! The Eagle Scout was perfect backup—resourceful, committed, drunk as hell. The night opened for them like a parted sea. Into the inky dark center of it they plunged.

. . .

Bedford Forrest lived to be 56, which is pretty good for a guy who purportedly had thirty horses shot out from beneath him as he fought to keep slaves enslaved.

Apart from the unchecked racism, though, he really wasn't that unlike my big brother. Both uneducated yet successful, tough as hell, strong leaders and a little crazy (or maybe a lot). Both careening through life on seemingly borrowed time. Surviving. Nathan having died only to be memorialized on over thirty historical markers in Tennessee alone. My big brother thirty-years-old, goddamit, creeping through the night with a handsaw and a rope, on a mission, dead set on celebrating life by tearing something down—a sacrifice, perhaps, an offering to the gods for his warm, still-strong body coursing with blood after all those years.

My brother and the Eagle Scout found the unmarked gravel access to the memorial, snuck past all the chain link fence and barbed wire, got down on their bellies and began sawing with pruning saws at the ankles of the horse. The serrated blades sliced through the fiberglass and foam easily, but then hit an unexpected metal—a steel skeleton to keep the statue upright amidst high winds and attempted vandalism.

No matter. They took a ¾ inch bull rope, the one used to lift entire trees off the ground, and tied it around the statue with a running bowline knot and snuck out of the compound, uncoiling as they went. There was a rail-line nearby, a busy one where freight trains screeched by with their cargo every half hour.

And now they were giddy and laughing, crawling military style until they reached the rails, and then my brother hopped over and tied the other end of the rope to a tree, stretching it taut across the tracks so when the next train came it would catch the rope and rip the statue away.

The excitement was almost too much for them, the perfection of their plan, envisioning the general and his horse yanked from their foundation and bouncing along the train tracks toward Chattanooga.

And then a train came, began a painfully slow approach around the corner, closing in on the rope. But the engineer saw. It's as if it was someone's job to scout ahead for such booby traps and stop the train in time. A uniformed man hopped out and walked up to the rope, yanked on it a little, shook his head and then sliced it away with a knife. And he had a flashlight, the beam of which he lowered along the ditch in a slow, deliberate side-to-side.

My brother and the Eagle Scout had held their breath too long. They erupted from their hiding places and ran like hell, unsure if the uniformed man was following, the beam of light scraping across their backs, across their shoulders, they ran until they reached the car hidden further down the road. They cranked the key, hit the gas, and in a flash they were history.

I heard of the debacle from a distance, caught up in school and marriage, but I could imagine every movement, the looks on their faces, my brother's wild laugh. I could imagine the particular tenor of his voice when he gets excited with an alcohol-saturated idea, how his volume ratchets up and his words begin to slur. The rowdiness in his eyes.

I told my wife what they did and she said, "He's lucky he didn't get killed." And that's perhaps the story of his life. Luck, blessing, grace. I'm not sure what I believe for him anymore, or for me, but somehow he's maneuvered through his days with a kind of magic. Perhaps just mercy.

. . .

The statue is still there. But the attempt at removing it didn't go completely unnoticed. There was a small but vociferous uproar, an op-ed from a local columnist, Frank Ritter, decrying the vandalism as a hate crime:

> In the dead of night, someone invaded fenced-in private property here recently, tied a heavy rope around a statue after cutting its legs half-way through, then stretched the rope a hundred yards or so and attached it to a railroad track, apparently hoping a passing train would topple the heroic sculpture.

A blogger, Sister Bubba, while not quite defending the act, at least challenged the accusation of hate crime:

> "I can't go there. The murder of 3 civil rights workers is a hate crime. The bombing of a church in Birmingham, Alabama that killed 4 young girls is a hate crime. Tearing down a statue of a confederate general, regardless of motivation and bias, is a prank—granted a rather ill-conceived prank that for whatever reason, the perpetrator could not pull off (or pull down)."

For my brother and the Eagle Scout, the perpetrators, "ill-conceived prank" stung a little. It was a good plan, albeit conducted in a cloud of gin and adrenaline. Or maybe not a good plan. Perhaps someone could have died, or a train derailed. Perhaps it was criminal, reckless, but no, not a hate crime. Something to do, something big! A gift to oneself on a birthday that was never supposed to come.

. . .

Shortly after his Bedford Forrest birthday my brother began tattooing rings onto his shoulder, concentric circles opening out, reaching for the collar bone, a ring for each year of life he has lived like the crosscut map of a tree's history, some inked thick to reflect a year of joy and abundance, some thin with a season of grief and drought.

And when it is winter in Nashville he still rises every day, shakes the cold from his callused fingertips, breathes warmth onto his swollen knuckles and goes into the trees.

The Eagle Scout decided that to die is gain and headed to the jungles of Burma where he ferries relief supplies to displaced villagers under perpetual threat of attack from the Burmese army. He has a piece of leather stamped with the longitude and latitude of Sam Donald's old farm: 35° 56' 56" N   86° 41' 37 W. He wears it around his wrist to remind him of where he's been, where he comes from. He emails through a satellite once every few months. Tells us he's still alive.

Craig the part-time comic leapt from the top of the Parthenon Building in Nashville and died upon impact. His lungs were shot through with cancer. There was blood in his cough. Pain in his chest and back. He wanted to spare his ex-wife, his boy, the trauma of watching him die. He put it all to rest with one final flight.

Last I heard, Kenny was selling Ford trucks north of town. Thomas is still in the trees.

For my brother the birthdays keep coming and he marvels at each one, each new year like a gift he never asked for, never expected to receive.

And there is always this: the moments that part like a sea, so many of them, and all you have to do is walk into that corridor knowing the watery walls could crash in at any second, but it doesn't matter because each second is made better and more delicious by that tremendous plunge, into the center, and the hunger that moves you and the sound of all the rushing water— so many millions of tons—right at your ears.

That's what it was like to climb all those trees. That's what it felt like at those heights, reaching always for the next limb.

The Eagle Scout hears it now in the jungle, God bless him. Like a lion's roar. The stars like suspended fire, and the moon and planets.

I imagine Craig hearing it one more time, too.

And my big brother, warming his fingers by the woodstove at night, thinking through tomorrow's labor. His friends have died young and he has magicked into another year. He never thought he'd be here, more than a decade after eighteen.

Nathan Bedford Forrest still stands on Nashville's I-65, waves of traffic lapping at the half-sawed hooves of his horse. Some things simply persist. My brother's hands are cracked from the cold, blood coming through the skin, red as the parted sea.

Epilogue

—Freeville, New York

I see a curtain of sagging, sharp spruce branches in the front yard. The black tar road snakes just beyond, tiny dark bubbles expanding and popping because it's so hot. Like a tar pit, the kind that trapped all the saber tooth tigers and boiled them alive. When I walk across that road my shoes will stick, and I will carry the broken bubbles on my soles into the cornfield.

The cornfield is just past the road and lasts forever. It is taller than me, orderly and dark inside. The cornfield defies the laws of natural things. The streams around the field are not straight. The branches of the trees behind the field are crooked and snarled. The leaves fall randomly in clumps and even Mom's garden zigzags through the yard, nothing growing quite where it should. Things connected to dirt are not supposed to be straight.

Yet here is the corn, stalks rising from real earth, and when I press in among the shoots I see only perfect lines and perfect spacing. I bend to the ground and stare into the shadowy rows and when I position my face in front of the first stalk, I see only that one. The thousands behind it disappear in a perfect, uniform line. I inhale decay and bursting life all at the same time and my lungs are full.

But the cornfield is only in the way. An in-between. What matters most is arriving at the hazy silhouette of woods beyond the field, the shaggy treetops scratching at the horizon, a city of interlaced branches and birds and the trampled deer trails running beneath. It is my daily eight-year-old destination, my favorite place in the world. It is also a million miles away. A blacktop road and cornfield away. It feels like it takes forever to reach, walking steady through the stalks, whose leathery leaves draw blood as I pass by.

So I've invented a secret philosophy for the passage. I stand here in my yard, looking through the spruce branches, and when I see past the corn and into the woods I focus as hard as I can and think: it's only a matter of time before I'm *in those woods* looking back.

This is a marvel. Each time it goes heavy in my mind.

This current me, the one standing here without having taken a step, will in a flash become a future me, there, in the woods, thinking back to the beginning, imagining my clean-soled shoes and how far it seemed before I stepped across that field to the other side.

It is a connection of selves over the ether. It is time travel without the machine, my home-grown tesseract. All I have to do is start walking, stop, and then remember.

. . .

My secret philosophy works for more than just walks to the woods. I used it, for example, when my 3rd grade Love Inn teacher made my class eat olives. She wanted us to appreciate and understand the food of another culture.

"Mediterranean food is not like ours," she said. "It has much better flavor and is better for your body."

She swished a large jar of olives in front of us, a tiny tornado of green globes swirling in their own juice. They looked like pickled green eyes. I said I wouldn't eat them, that I would wait until next week when she brought in the food of Italy, which I assumed would be pasta or pizza.

But she insisted. "*Everyone* will eat an olive," she said. "*Everyone* will line up and take an olive on a toothpick and chew the thing until it gets into your tummy. These are good for you, kids. Welcome to Greece."

I saw the faces of my friends as the olives went into their mouths. They looked like someone ran over their toes with a bike. One classmate spit out her piece only to be told by the teacher that she had to try again until it was chewed and gone.

Greece was a horrible place.

But I had something up my sleeve. A secret philosophy up my sleeve. With every step toward the jar I reminded myself that in a breath I would be looking back at that event from the future. I would be in my room, or even better, at my kitchen table gorging on macaroni and cheese, and then I would remember that exact olive moment and think to myself: you're over. Finished. And here I am, safely on the other side.

It worked! I'm here in the yard and that olive is buried, although I think I can still taste it a little. My philosophy doesn't erase memories. It merely uses them. It takes a moment, shoots you forward, and when you look back you connect with the past you, pre-olive you, and you wink at yourself across time. Sometimes it takes your breath away.

...

From here in my yard I can see most of the world. Our neighbor Kermit's farm is endless, stretching to the east a million miles. And to the right, along the curvy blacktop road, I can see the top of the Hippy House, where I've been told not to go. The hippies swim naked in the pond, smoke things, and in general do a bad job of believing in Jesus as their personal Lord and Savior, which is Mom and Dad's most serious allegation against them. I can only see the second story of their house because they have let the shrubs grow up without any pruning. Their house is drowning in plant life, gasping through the green.

Mom and Dad have never said so plainly, but I get the feeling that the hippies are dirty people.

But they have a pond. It is oval and deep and the seasonal home to turtles and snakes. It is our skating rink in the winter and our swimming hole in the summer, but only after Mom has scouted the area and confirmed that the hippies are either fully clothed or inside their house, doing secret things.

The pond is where Trapper almost died—Trapper the

Springer Spaniel who loves water as much as he loves squirrels and rolling in dead things. He loves water so much that one day he jumped off the dock and right into a mess of rowboat ropes and cattails that tangled around his legs and trapped him. He was going under. I saw him from the dock but I had a lump of fear in my throat so big I couldn't even scream.

So I used my secret philosophy. I thought that in just a few minutes Future Me would look back at that exact moment and, unless I jumped in to save my dog, Future Me would not wink at or high-five Past Me. There would be a lot of tension between the two Me's, a falling out. If I didn't get in that pond right now and save my dog, it would be like someone yanked out all the wires on my time machine and messed up all the settings. Regret, or something even worse—something that couldn't catch its breath, even in that enormous air between—would become the monkey wrench in the motor of the machine.

I jumped. I freed Trapper's limbs from the ropes and tore away the cattails. I screamed and wrestled and tried to keep my head above water. He dug his claws into my chest and left red welts but he was only trying to survive.

When he finally swam back to shore and walked into the grass, he shook the pond water from his fur and looked as if nothing happened. I sat down in the dirt and he came over to lick my face. I thought of Past Me on the dock, the one who was so scared, the one who was squinting into *right now* and shaking, trying to put that desperate message in a bottle for Future Me.

I closed my eyes, concentrated, and in my mind gave Past Me a bone-rattling high five. "Future Me is okay," I whispered. "Still breathing, still tethered. So proud of you."

…

I see my yard all around me. It's huge. Five acres. We used to play lawn darts right over there before they started killing people and became illegal. We switched to weighted Styrofoam darts and stopped worrying that the cops would catch us on their way to arrest the hippies.

My house is behind me, three stories tall, a former hotel during the 1800's and built like a tank to withstand earthquakes or hurricanes or invasions from the Prussian army. It has a wood-burning furnace in the basement that shoots heat through the house and into our blankets, which we teepee over ourselves and the vents to capture the warmth.

Mom's asparagus meanders outside. It crowds into the beets and overlaps with the carrots. It has evicted the tomatoes to an entirely different section of the garden and unfortunately sneaks all the way into our kitchen and onto my dinner plate.

And beyond the garden is where the creek winds into town. When the weekends are nice, my family pulls out the vacuum cleaner, reverses the suction and pumps up the rafts and floats down the creek until we get to the general store, which is where we buy beef jerky and little cardboard containers of ice cream with attached wooden spoons. We surrender to the current and drift and it's a rare thing if someone doesn't get tipped into the creek. That is our favorite thing: the tipping over.

This yard is a universe. And it was right here that I told my brother about my secret philosophy, looking through the spruce branches and explaining the mechanics of it. He was amazed. Especially when we tried it, walking through the corn to the edge of the woods and turning back to the house. He closed his eyes, thought of Past Aaron who hadn't even taken a step, and connected.

"It works," he whispered.

That's when I told him about the name.

"It's called *Moments in History*," I said. "*M in H*, for short. It's a secret, but you can use it if you want."

. . .

There have been times I've tried to make *M in H* work the opposite way, to slow things down and freeze a moment, to trap it in ice like the wooly mammoths. Sometimes there's a day that's so perfect and sunny and grassy that you want to slow it all down and stop future moments from coming so soon. Suddenly the in-between matters most. You want to lie in the grass and watch planes slicing the sky and imagine how much God must love the sky to always erase the smoke and bring back the blue.

But I most wanted to freeze that day when Mom brought a lamb onto the seat in the bay window because it was dying. She had a bottle in its mouth and ran her hand over its belly, which was rising and falling with its breath, softer and softer.

She said it was going to die. She said she couldn't do anything to save it. That's when I tried the hardest to stop time, to freeze that moment when there was still a little life in the lamb. I would have sacrificed Future Me and my whole philosophy if I could have kept the warm breath inside the baby, and Mom's hand riding its belly like a wave.

. . .

To be honest, many decades have flittered away since Mom held that lamb—a long string of years separate me from the olives and Trapper, my floating family and Mom in her garden, tending her vegetables. Mom and Dad have drifted apart, and a whole host of animals, including Trapper, have gone into the ground, most at the end of my own shovel.

I've brought my wife back to this place, to this exact spot in the yard, to show her the view and to give her a glimpse of me when I was a little boy. She said she wanted to see it, to better understand the man she chose to marry.

"Past Me used to think about you a lot," I say.

But the view has changed, as it tends to do. The curtain of spruce, the first trees to form a kind of woody fence around me, has been cut down, and when I turn to see the three hulking stories of my house I find an empty patch of grass. The whole structure was long ago severed from its foundation, lifted onto two giant trucks and carted a half mile up the road just beyond the Hippy House which, abandoned, is now completely covered in green. The asparagus is gone too, and all the traces of my family's life in this place are locked in our heads and hearts, floating down separate tributaries, some more tumultuous than others.

But the woods are still here, just over the blacktop and past the cornfield. Within them is the junkyard where my brother and I used to roam. And as much as I've tried to forget it, the salt of every olive still seems vivid on my tongue. And here we are, my wife and I, our toes poised over the same blacktop. I'm explaining *M in H*, how it works and how it doesn't. I tell her that when I was a kid all I wanted to do was get past the cornfield and into the woods. To the trees. It was a long way and I figured a secret philosophy would help take off some of the journey's edge. But I never imagined it would lead me back here, as a so-called grown-up, a person who buys kale and keeps his receipts for tax purposes, a married man more world-weary than he cares to admit, and that all those moments in between, the staccato inhale and exhale of so many Past Me's, would lead to this present. I never quite thought this far ahead, or considered the swirl of circumstances that might land me here.

My wife takes my hand and points past the cornfield. "In just a few moments we'll be in those woods," she says. "Looking back."

And she's right. In just a few moments we'll be in those woods, and in a few more we'll be parents and then grandparents, looking back. In just a few moments we'll be ancient, a hundred years old, severed from a hundred foundations and standing on dirt filled with the graves of our pets and people, looking back.

She says she is ready. We take a step and then another. We stop. We remember. It takes our breath away.

Acknowledgments and Admissions

The genesis of this project feels ancient and includes friends and family now distant, some deceased, alongside a list of influences and supporters it would be impossible to include here. A more contemporary shortlist might begin with the generous support of Joyce Munro, Nancy Thomas, Christine Bayles Kortsch, Philip Gerard, Wendy Brenner, David Gessner, John Jeremiah Sullivan, Sarah Messer, Diana Hume George, Peter Trachtenberg, Rebecca Lee, Clyde Edgerton, Phil Furia, Rod McClain, Annie Bellerose, Doug Diesenhaus, and Amanda Gonzales, as well as current colleagues Mathew Gavin Frank, Jon Billman, Jen Howard, Jason Markle, Dan Gocella, Matt Bell, Zac Cogley and Andrea Scarpino. The Andersens and MacIvors are remarkable clans now fused by a single hyphen, and I'm endlessly grateful for the love and support of both, and particularly for my partner, Kathryn, who has believed in me and my words ever since she crested that hill. Journals and magazines who published earlier incarnations of this book include *Gulf Coast, Fourth Genre, Ruminate, Rock and Sling, Arts and Letters, Northwest Review, Memoir (and), Paris Review (Daily), Sycamore Review, The Drum, New Millennium Writings, Diagram, Sojourners,* and *Catapult Magazine.* The indented text on page 184 is from the Wendell Berry poem, "Manifesto: The Mad Farmer Liberation Front," and the Ryszard Kapuscinski text in chapter 7 is from the book *Imperium.* I am deeply indebted to Eric Rutkow for his brilliant work of history, *American Canopy: Trees, Forests, and the Making of a Nation,* which was invaluable as I tried to map North American tree hunger. Lastly, this is a work of memory and interpretation, both of which are intimately my own. While it is mostly nonfiction, a few names have been changed and the chronology of events, as well as some details, have been shaped for the sake of the story.

About the author

Josh MacIvor-Andersen is an award-winning writer, teacher, and tree climber. He lives on the shores of a (superior) Great Lake with his partner, Kathryn, two wild, curious, holistically kick-ass children, and a fat cat named Baby Kitty.